A Quest for Biblical Theology

Jan Barna

(Editor)

A Quest for Biblical Theology

Festschrift in Honour of Gunnar Pedersen

Newbold Academic Press

Editor: Jan Barna

Copy-editors: John Baildam, Jonquil Hole

Layout: Manfred Lemke, NAP

Cover graphic: Any Kobel, Switzerland

Printing: INGRAM SPARK

© Newbold Academic Press, 2024
Bracknell
Berkshire RG42 4AN
United Kingdom
newbold.ac.uk

Except as otherwise permitted under the Copyright, Designs and Patents Act 1988 this publication may only be reproduced, stored or transmitted in any form or by any means, with the prior permission of the publisher, or in the case of reprographic reproduction, in accordance with the terms of a licence issued by The Copyright Licensing Agency. Enquiries concerning reproduction outside those terms should be sent to Newbold Academic Press, Bracknell, Berkshire, RG42 4AN, United Kingdom.

ISBN 978-1-9162888-1-2, Softcover

Contents

Part 1

Biblical Studies Perspectives

On the Road to Gaza: A Biblical Paradigm for Hermeneutics   19
   Jean-Claude Verrecchia

What if God is Absent? The Challenge of Incorporating Esther
into a Biblical Theology   41
   Laurence A. Turner

To Eat or Not To Eat: Food and Hubris in Daniel   57
   Ivan Milanov

Living in the Post-Easter Era: The Theology of the Matthean
Eschatological Discourse (Matthew 24-25)   67
   Laszlo Gallusz

Part 2

Reflective Perspectives

The Right Thing to Do: A Reflection on Navigating the
Complexities of Everyday Moral Choices   85
   Michael Pearson

In His Will Is Our Peace: 97
   Radisa Antic

Teaching and Preaching Adventist Core Beliefs in a
Postmodern Context   107
   Rolf J. Pöhler

Part 3

Theological Perspectives

Our Place in God's Story: Towards a Narrative Ecclesiology   119
   Tihomir Lazic

Context, Issues and Future of Adventist Hermeneutics   139
   Jan Barna

A Search for the Biblical Epistemic Horizon: Towards Meta-Hermeneutics   171
   Gunnar Pedersen and Jan Barna

Contributors

Radisa Antic, PhD, is Principal Lecturer Emeritus in Systematic Theology at Newbold College of Higher Education and former Director of the Ellen G. White Research Centre at Newbold.

Jan Barna, PhD, is Principal Lecturer in Systematic and Biblical Theology and Head of Research at Newbold College of Higher Education.

Laszlo Gallusz, PhD, is Principal Lecturer in New Testament Studies and Head of the Centre for Ministry and Mission at Newbold College of Higher Education.

Tihomir Lazic, DPhil, is Senior Lecturer in Theology at Newbold College of Higher Education.

Ivan Milanov, PhD, is Senior Lecturer in Old Testament Studies and Director of Postgraduate Programmes at Newbold College of Higher Education.

Michael Pearson, DPhil, is Principal Lecturer Emeritus in Ethics at Newbold College of Higher Education.

Gunnar Pedersen, ThD, is Principal Lecturer Emeritus in Systematic and Biblical Theology at Newbold College of Higher Education.

Prof. Rolf Pöhler, ThD, is Professor Emeritus in Systematic Theology at Theologische Hochschule Friedensau in Germany.

Laurence Turner, PhD, is Principal Lecturer Emeritus in Old Testament Studies at Newbold College of Higher Education.

Jean-Claude Verrecchia, Docteur ès sciences religieuses, is Principal Lecturer Emeritus in New Testament Studies, Hermeneutics, and Second Temple Judaism at Newbold College of Higher Education.

Foreword

It has been an honour to work on this celebratory book to commemorate the contribution of Dr Gunnar Pedersen to Adventist theology. During his years as pastor, administrator and educator, Gunnar has touched and influenced the lives of many people with whom he came in contact. I have been privileged to know Gunnar as his doctoral student, my colleague and mentor. It is my and the other contributors' pleasure to present this *Festschrift* volume to Gunnar himself to commemorate his distinctive contribution to a wider readership. May this be to him a reminder of his calling from God and of his unique gifts and fruits of the Spirit which the Church has recognised and has come to value greatly.

Gunnar Pedersen's educational and theological contributions have become some of the most important in the field of systematic and biblical theology in both European and global Adventism. Gunnar has been working predominantly in the field of *biblical* systematic theology, as opposed to philosophical, dogmatic, applied or historical systematic theology fields. His main input has been transforming systematic theology at Newbold College of Higher Educatio, which up until the mid-1990s used to offer classes in this field which were of a dogmatic (proof-text based) and historical-philosophical nature, into classes which reflected his conviction for the possibility of having systematic theology which is holistic, biblical, canonical and narrative in essence and form. To this end, Gunnar's latest published contribution 'A Search for the Biblical Epistemic Horizon: Towards Meta-Hermeneutics' (republished here as the last chapter of the book) excellently demonstrates the heart of his lifelong academic contribution. Gunnar has helpfully started to distinguish between Biblical Theology proper, providing core thematic structure, language and overall narrative framework, and Systematic Theology, which, as an applied discipline, should be providing modern articulations of biblical themes. Gunnar has put the two to work together as two sides of the same coin. This is not only a unique and important contribution to Adventist systematic theology, but also to systematic theology and to biblical theology in general.

At this point a few lines about the organisation of the book may be appropriate in aiding the reader to navigate its pages more easily. The book is split into three parts which cover ten chapters. Part One explores questions of Biblical Hermeneutics and Biblical Theology from the perspective of Old and New Testament Studies. There are four chapters in this section starting with Jean-Claude Verrecchia's explorative chapter about a biblical paradigm for hermeneutics, followed by Laurence Turner's discussion on the challenge of incorporating Esther into Biblical Theology. These are further followed by Ivan Milanov's offering of a biblical exposition of eating and not eating in Daniel 1 and the section concludes with Laszlo Gallusz's proposal for a coherent theology of the famous Matthean eschatological discourse of chapters 24 and 25.

The middle section of the *Festschrift* contains three insightful chapters of varied nature starting with Michael Pearson's reflective chapter about the complexities of everyday moral decisions, followed by Radisa Antic's contemplative reading of Ecclesiastes and concluding with Rolf Pöhler's thoughtful chapter about teaching and preaching Adventist core beliefs in a postmodern context.

Part Three concludes the book with three chapters. These come from Gunnar's colleagues in the fields of systematic theology. The section starts with an innovative chapter by Tihomir Lazic, on using Biblical Theology for a narrative Ecclesiology. This is followed by a chapter by Jan Barna about the context, issues and future of Adventist hermeneutics and the section, as well as the book, is concluded with Gunnar's own contribution to the field of Biblical Theology. The last chapter is thematically connected with and, in some ways, can be seen as a continuation of the previous chapter. It is about the necessity of the meta-hermeneutics of Biblical Theology for hearing the biblical horizon of the Bible–a theme that effectively summarises Gunnar's life-long academic efforts.

This book has been prepared with the desire to acknowledge properly not only Gunnar's unique academic-teaching contribution to, but also his extensive personal-educational and pastoral-leadership impact on, the life and the mission of the Seventh-day Adventist Church. Gunnar has influenced many generations of students at Newbold College of Higher Education, who in turn have become pastors, teachers and leaders in many countries in Europe and far beyond. All those who have worked and brushed shoulders with Gunnar would agree that in the first place they encountered in Gunnar a capable theologian, whose eloquently captivating talks and refreshing analyses were the natural extensions of his genuine and humble personality. To all who came to know him personally and closely–this is who Gunnar is: a humble yet brilliant giant.

At this point thanks also have to be expressed not only to the contributors of the book's chapters, but also to Dr John Baildam for his proof-reading and style editing of the chapters. Unfortunately, John's work on the Festschrift proved to be his last contribution as John passed away just before the book could be finished and printed. As the editor of the book, I'd like to acknowledge John's extensive and excellent contribution to the *Festschrift*. Not only was working with him very efficient, but the level of his feedback was exceptional and made the work of the editor much easier. The final book is therefore what it is, thanks to John's professional and excellent contribution too. Newbold College and Newbold Academic Press will greatly miss John Baildam and his impact on NAP and its publications.

In order to create a meaningful context to Gunnar's academic contribution we provide a brief overview of the main turning points of Gunnar's life and ministry, after which his dedication to God and his mission is captured in a personal narrative by his life-companion Lisbeth.

Gunnar was born on 13 March 1943 in Denmark. He was a student at Danish Junior College, Vejlefjord, between 1961 and 1963, also having been pre-admitted to Newbold College. Gunnar then went on to serve as a Bible Worker between 1964 and 1965 and from 1965 he became a student at Newbold College where he graduated with a diploma in theology on 7 May 1967, soon followed by the full degree of Columbia Union College's Bachelor of Arts programme on 5 August 1967.

After his initial exposure to formal theological education, Gunnar began to work as pastor in Hillerød church and co-worker in Copenhagen in 1968 and 1969 as well as pastor of Slagelse and Næstved churches between 1968 and 1970.

Gunnar's second stint in formal higher education unfolded between 1970 and 1972 during which time he became a student at Andrews University, USA, where he graduated with a Master of Divinity degree on 17 August 1972.

Gunnar's next steps led him back to ministry in Denmark where he became a youth leader in the East Danish Conference. His call to ministry was officially recognised by the Church on 9 August 1975 when he was ordained to gospel ministry.

After these pastoral ministry years, Gunnar turned to higher education once again. He started to advance his education and after being encouraged by his professors, including Raoul Dederen, he took classes in the Doctor of Theology programme at the Seventh-day Adventist Theological Seminary at Andrews University between 1976 and 1979.

In 1979 he then returned to Denmark to Skodsborg Sanatorium where he worked as pastor and Bible teacher for students at the Physiotherapy School. He remained in this role until 1981, in which year Gunnar took a leave of absence to write his dissertation—yet he also continued to mentor a young pastor in Odense, Denmark.

Between 1986 and 1992 Gunnar worked as pastor for Vejlefjord Church and as Bible teacher at Vejlefjord Junior College from where he was called to become the Danish Union President, a role in which he served between 1992 and 1995.

Gunnar graduated with a Doctor of Theology (ThD) degree from Andrews University on 2 June 1996. His dissertation provided a ground-breaking study in the difficult area between Protestant soteriology and Adventist eschatology: 'The Soteriology of Ellen G. White Compared with the Lutheran Formula of Concord: A Study of the Adventist Doctrine of the Final Judgement of the Saints and Their Justification Before God.'

In 1995 Gunnar was called to teach at Newbold College where he taught classes in systematic and biblical theology until he moved back to Denmark in 2012. Gunnar's seventeen years spent at the leading higher education institution in the Trans-European Division provided in many ways the climax to and the fruition of his spiritual gifts. During these seventeen years Gunnar was also the head of the theology department for several years.

Since retiring to Denmark in 2012 Gunnar has continued to teach classes as Principal Lecturer Emeritus. In addition, it appears that Gunnar's retirement has been mostly on paper, since beyond teaching at Newbold, he has also has lectured in Croatia, South Africa, Serbia and Russia.

Significantly, Gunnar has prepared and presented around thirty lectures about the 'Great Story' or Biblical Theology's meta-narrative, which have been professionally recorded both in Danish and English for wide usage. In his retirement Gunnar has not shied away from invitations to preach and present seminars whenever he has been asked, always motivated by his own divine-call motto: 'If anybody wants to hear about God, I will try to be there.'

In the final part of the *Foreword,* readers will find a unique personal perspective by Gunnar's wife Lisbeth, without whom Gunnar would not be the blessing he has become to so many.

> Gunnar was a student at Vejlefjord Academy when he realised the need for God's word to be told, and although he did not believe that he was cut out for ministry, he nevertheless enrolled in a programme designed to prepare students for theological studies and went on to complete a BA in Theology at Newbold College.
>
> Soon after entering ministry, he realised that he needed to expand his knowledge in order to sufficiently fulfil the needs of the churches. With this in mind, he enrolled at Andrews University for more in-depth studies of God's Word, and graduated in 1972 with a Master of Divinity degree.
>
> After once again pastoring in Denmark for a couple of years, Gunnar returned to Andrews University for further theological studies. Strongly encouraged by his professors to complete a Doctor of Theology, he went on to complete the classes required, but then money ran out, and he returned to Denmark to pastor while at the same time working on his doctoral thesis. Thus in 1996 Gunnar graduated from Andrews University with a Doctor of Theology degree.
>
> When Newbold College contacted him and asked him to come and teach, Gunnar was serving as President of the Danish Union of Churches. His answer was that he would take the position, but only after having completed his term as president in full, and that Newbold College was entirely free to employ someone else instead, if they felt the need to. Only after thus faithfully fulfilling his promise to the Danish Union did he go on to teach at

Newbold, where he had quite a few busy but very fulfilling years in the theology department.

Gunnar and his wife, Lisbeth, have two children, a daughter and a son, and three grandchildren. At Newbold they were joined by both children with their families. Their son-in-law and daughter-in-law completed their theological studies and are now pastoring in the Adventist Church in Denmark.

Gunnar is a fantastic and faithful husband, a loving father and grandfather. He is a dedicated pastor and teacher, who continually keeps himself updated on what is going on in the world and in the world of theology in particular. He is ever learning and exploring, continually purchasing new literature, always improving his lectures and teaching resources, and never merely repeating former lessons or lectures.

But more importantly, we who are closest to Gunnar know that his number one priority is spending time with the God he loves. He is continually–night and day–in prayer for his family, his Church and not least every one of his students.

Thank you, Gunnar, for teaching us about Jesus' faithfulness and showing us what faithfulness to God looks like.

Jan Barna, March 2024

Part 1
Biblical Studies Perspectives

On the Road to Gaza: A Biblical Paradigm for Hermeneutics

Jean-Claude Verrecchia

Introduction

When Stephen was arrested and hauled by the mob before the council, he probably did not expect that this appearance before the highest Jewish authorities would end fatally (Acts 7). This man, full of grace and power, was dragged out of Jerusalem and stoned. Not only did he become the first Christian martyr, but the persecution which followed, led by Saul, scattered all the believers except the apostles throughout Judea and Samaria (Acts 8:1).

These dramatic circumstances produced a radical shift from a centripetal geography whose centre was Jerusalem,[1] to a centrifugal geography whose boundaries were no less than the ends of the earth. Whereas the gospel of Luke had started and ended in Jerusalem (Luke 1.8ff.; 24:52), now the book of Acts departs from Jerusalem and turns towards foreign territories (Acts 1:4; 28:23ff.). Multiple journeys occur, in many stages. The last paragraph of the book of Acts describes Paul settled in his own house in Rome, the capital of the Roman empire. Jesus' words are fulfilled: the gospel has reached the ends of the earth (Acts 1:8).

Samaria was the first stage of this geographical deployment. Philip, one of the seven, a colleague of Stephen, is the main character in two episodes. The

---

1 See Jesus deliberately making his way to Jerusalem: Luke 9:51, 53; 10:38; 13:22, 33; 14:25; 17:11; 19:28.

aim of this contribution is to focus on the second one (Acts 8:26-40), in which Philip meets an Ethiopian on his way back home after having come to Jerusalem to worship.

Commentators disagree concerning the role and purpose of this pericope. For Hans Conzelmann, it is an isolated episode, whose function is to serve as a prelude (*Präludium*)[2] to the story of Cornelius (Acts 10). Frederick Bruce considers that 'if it were removed, there would be nothing to indicate that anything of the kind had ever stood there'.[3] A significant group of interpreters asserts that this story works as a mission narrative *(Missionerzählung* or *Missionschema)*.[4] Differently, *The Reformation Commentary on Scripture* affirms that this text highlights 'the complexity of *sola Scriptura*' contrary to the *claritas scripturae* claimed by Luther.[5] For Craig Keener the pericope is a 'proleptic fulfilment of 1:8'. According to the geographical sequence set in Jesus' words, after Samaria, the gospel should reach the 'ends of the earth'. Yet Philip did not travel so far away, as he meets on the road to Gaza a representative of this remote world.[6] In this encounter, the Ethiopian is the prototype of a pious god-seeker, and the core meaning of the account is paradigmatic.[7] Following this line of thought, Marianne Kartzow points to more recent interpretations focusing on the complex identity and the 'otherness' of the Ethiopian. She explains why such a narrative has raised a hermeneutical interest and 'has also been brought to the fore by feminist, gay and lesbian groups as active practitioners in religious communities,

---

2   Hans Conzelmann, *Die Apostelgeschichte* (Tübingen: JCB Mohr, 1963), 63.
3   Frederick F. Bruce, 'Philip and the Ethiopian', JJS 34 (1989): 378.
4   See for example Rudolf Pesch, *Die Apostelgeschichte* (Apg 1-12), (Evangelisch-Katholischer Kommentar zum Neuen Testament; Zürich: Benziger Verlag, 1986), 287; Josef Zmijewski, Die Apostelgeschichte (Regensburger Neues Testament; Regensburg: Verlag Friedrich Pustet, 1994), 360.
5   *Reformation Commentary on Scripture*, vol. VI, Acts, 113, ed. by Esther Chung-Kim and Todd R. Hains (Downers Grove: IVP, 2014). For Calvin, numerous aids have been provided by the Lord for understanding the good news. It is therefore important to have a teachable spirit willing to ask others for help.
6   Cf. Craig S. Keener, Acts. *An Exegetical Commentary*, 3:1-14:28, vol. 2 (Grand Rapids: Baker, 2013), 1534.
7   Cf. Gottfried Schille, *Die Apostelgeschichte des Lukas* (Theologischer Handkommentar zum Neuen Testament 5; Berlin: Evangelische Verlagsanstalt, 1983), 215; Jürgen Roloff, *Die Apostelgeschichte* (Das Neue Testament Deutsch 5; Göttingen: Vandenhoeck & Ruprecht, 1981), 139.

in search of narratives that may provide religious figures to identify with, and that can provide material for preaching from a gay and lesbian perspective'.[8]

This paper asserts that beyond the traditional missiological interpretations of the text, the encounter between Philip and the Ethiopian provides a biblical paradigm for hermeneutics, as it offers, long before Schleiermacher and the like, answers to the still pending question: what does it mean to understand? The paper will develop in two parts. First, it will provide an exegetical analysis of the pericope;[9] second, it will re-read the text from a hermeneutical point of view.

Exegesis

Context

The encounter between Philip and the Ethiopian eunuch belongs to a long section, running from Acts 8:1 to 11:18, containing four conversion stories: the Samaritans' (Acts 8: 4-25); the eunuch's (Acts 8:26-40); Saul's (Acts 9:1-19); Cornelius's (Acts 10:1-48). When Philip arrives in the city of Samaria, he is on the fringes of Judaism. There is no intermediate stage, mentioning a mission in Judea, as expected from Jesus' set itinerary: from Jerusalem, 'in all Judea and Samaria' (Acts 1:8). Even Peter and John, the emissaries of the apostles, on their way back to Jerusalem proclaim the good news 'to many villages of the Samaritans' (Acts 8:25). As for the story of the Ethiopian, it is geographically at odds. It occurs not in Samaria, but on a desert road, somewhere in the wilderness (Acts 8:26). The Ethiopian is in-between: not in Jerusalem anymore, and not yet back home in his country. This is the first conversion of an individual, after the mass conversions during and soon after the Pentecost. Saul's conversion

---

8   Marianne B. Kartzow, 'Complex Identities: Ethnicity, Gender and Religion in the Story of the Ethiopian Eunuch (Acts 8:26-40),' *Religion & Theology* 17 (2010): 187.

9   Due to space constraints, this paper does not provide a detailed exegesis. It should be read as an incentive for further research. For a detailed exegesis, see Frederick F. Bruce, *The Acts of the Apostles* (Grand Rapids: Eerdmans, 1951); Pesch, *Die Apostelgeschichte* (Apg 1-12), 1986; Zmijewski, *Die Apostelgeschichte*, 1994; Daniel Marguerat, *Les Actes des Apôtres* (1-12), (Commentaire du Nouveau Testament Va; Genève: Labor et Fides, 2007); Richard I. Pervo, *Acts*, Hermeneia (Minneapolis: Fortress, 2009); Keener, Acts. *An Exegetical Commentary*, 3:1-4:28, vol. 2, 2013.

occurs in the suburbs of Damascus, 200 miles away from Jerusalem. As far as the fourth conversion's narrative is concerned, it occurs in Caesarea, the headquarters of the Roman empire in Judea, the harbour connecting the province with the Roman empire. Luke's account does not use the terminology of conversion for the Roman centurion Cornelius. He is clearly presented as a believer, praying constantly to God, generous, well-spoken of by the whole Jewish nation, eager to listen to the Lord.[10] In fact, this centurion is used as a tool in God's hands to lead Peter to a new understanding, in which he acknowledges that God now shows no partiality (Acts 10:34). The focus of this narrative lies mainly in the coming of the Holy Spirit upon the whole audience, yet another mass event.

Four narratives, each one located outside of Jerusalem. Four narratives, each one crossing the boundaries of normality. For it is abnormal for the good news to reach Samaria, whose inhabitants are at the same time close to Israel but quite opposed to Jerusalem. It is abnormal that Saul of Tarsus, the Jew, chief persecutor of the religious authorities, is called to preach the good news. It is abnormal that a Roman centurion is God's preferred intermediary to lead Peter to his new understanding. As for the Ethiopian eunuch, the exegesis will show how he is a paragon of abnormality.

Literary Genre

The huge and recent explosion of the travel industry has also had an impact on theological studies. Tour operators offer multiple trips to biblical countries and sites. Most translations of the Bible now include colour maps and topographical indexes. On the internet, the tribulations of Israel after leaving Egypt are tentatively reconstructed, as well as the various journeys of Paul. The work to Theophilus is probably the most conducive to this geographical interest. That the gospel of Luke is centripetal and the book of Acts is centrifugal is not disputed today. But the interpretation of Luke's obvious interest in travels varies. Where does it come from? To what end?

Richard Pervo claims that Luke's use of the travel motif comes directly from Greek novels.[11] Loveday Alexander asserts that Greek romance is such a large

---

10   Cf. Acts 10:2, 22, 33.
11   Richard I. Pervo, *Profit with Delight. The Literary Genre of the Acts of the Apostles* (Augsburg: Augsburg Press, 1987).

and complex phenomenon, that a comparison between Greek novels and Acts is necessary to understand the possible weight and value of this motif. Her analysis shows that sea crossing was important for the Greek novelists. She rightly notes that only Paul and his co-workers faced the challenge of sea crossing.[12] As there is no sea crossing in the Ethiopian narrative, the Greek novel model is therefore not helpful. In her conclusion, Alexander rather points to 'the *periplous* literature, with its pragmatic attention to detail, rather than the novels'.[13]

Daniel Marguerat extends the analysis of the travel motif into a taxonomy of six categories of travels: the tour, the founding of colonies, the exploratory journey, the romantic voyage, the philosopher's itinerary, and the initiatory journey.[14] Though this taxonomy sheds significant light on the book of Acts, and provides a valuable key to its understanding, the Ethiopian eunuch's narrative offers a specific situation, compared to the many travels in the book of Acts. While Paul is the main character, with his co-worker team, travelling to Asia, Greece, Italy, even Spain, here the main traveller is a foreigner who comes from Ethiopia to Jerusalem. While Paul is a centrifugal character, the Ethiopian is a centripetal one.

Intertextuality

Etienne Trocmé noted many correspondences between the Elijah/Elisha cycle and the Ethiopian pericope, especially in 1 Kings 18.[15] But other than references to the Mount Carmel confrontation, 2 Kings 2 and 5 offer better comparable data. Naaman the Syrian commander compares with the Ethiopian court officer (2 Kgs 5). The role of water is key in the two narratives. Elijah ascends into heaven (2 Kgs 2.11), whereas Philip is snatched away by the Spirit of the Lord (Acts 8:39). A connection with the prophet Zephaniah (2-3) has also been

---

12 Cf. Loveday Alexander, 'In Journeyings Often': Voyaging in the Acts of the Apostles and in Greek Romance, *JSNT* Sup 116, (Sheffield: Sheffield Academic Press, 1995), 37.
13 Loveday Alexander, 'Narrative Maps: Reflections on the Toponymy of Acts', in *The Bible in Human Society. Essays in Honour of John Rogerson*; JSOT 200 (Sheffield: Sheffield University Press, 1995), 41.
14 Daniel Marguerat, *La première histoire du christianisme. Les Actes des apôtres* (Paris : Cerf, 2007), 355.
15 Etienne Trocmé, *Le 'Livre des Actes' et l'histoire* (EHPR 45 ; Paris, Presses Universitaires de France, 1957), 180.

considered.¹⁶ The weight of these various elements does not seem sufficient to establish a strict intertextuality. At most, one can consider that Luke appropriates images and motifs from the prophetic tradition. On the other hand, a comparison between Jesus' encounter with the disciples on the road to Emmaus and Acts 8:26-40 is quite illuminating. The narrative unfolding is identical:

- The disciples and the Ethiopian leave Jerusalem (Luke 24:13/Acts 8:28)
- Question of the interpreter (Luke 24:17/Acts 8:30)
- Misunderstanding: the disciples are foolish/the Ethiopian does not understand (Luke 24:25/Acts 8:31)
- Interpretation of the Scriptures pointing to Jesus (Luke 24:27, 45/Acts 8:35)
- Sacramental action: Lord's Supper/baptism (Luke 24:42-43/Acts 8:38)
- Sudden disappearance of the interpreter (Luke 24:51/Acts8:39)
- Emotions: burning heart/joy (Luke 24:32/Acts 8:39)
- Continuation of the journey (Luke 24:52/Acts 8:39-40).

This comparison shows that Philip walks in the footsteps of his master. He comes to meet a God-seeker, somehow desperate due to his lack of understanding. He provides the explanatory development needed, focusing on his master's saving role.

Hearing the Text

Ben Witherington's book *New Testament Rhetoric* starts with this obvious statement: 'Jesus never said "let those who have eyes read", but "let those who have ears, listen"'.¹⁷ It follows that special attention should be given to sounds, as earlier stated by Paul Achtemeier: 'Organization of written materials ... depend[s] on sound rather than sight.'¹⁸ Although this importance of sound is widely recognised today, in practice biblical commentators are still much interested in

---

16   Cf. Richard I. Pervo, *Acts*, 220, especially Table 4. Zephaniah 2-3 and Acts 8 share some relevant words: μεσημβρίαν, Ἄζωτον, Αἰθίοψ.
17   Ben Witherington III, *New Testament Rhetoric. An Introductory Guide to the Art of Persuasion in and of the New Testament* (Eugene: Cascade, 2009), 1.
18   Paul J. Achtemeier, "Omne Verbum Sonat': The New Testament and the Oral Environment of Late Western Antiquity', *JBL* 109 (1990): 19.

considering texts as written documents. The grammar of sound developed by Margaret Lee and Brandon Scott opens new perspectives for biblical exegesis. Our subsequent exegesis, in line with this trend, therefore focuses on sounds, in particular beginning and ending sounds, sound patterns, and thematic sounds.[19]

Beginning and Ending Sounds

The pericope begins with these words: πορεύου ... ἐπὶ τὴν ὁδὸν (v. 26), reappearing twice: ὡς δὲ ἐπορεύοντο κατὰ τὴν ὁδόν (v. 36); ἐπορεύετο γὰρ τὴν ὁδὸν αὐτοῦ (v. 39). They all use the word ὁδός. Clearly, the beginning and ending sounds point to itinerancy as the main topic of the narrative. A close analysis of those repetitions is telling. Similarities are important. But dissimilarities are also significant. The first road mentioned is descending: τὴν καταβαίνουσαν. Likewise, in the second occurrence the road is going down; κατὰ τὴν ὁδόν. The last occurrence features with no preposition, but instead with the possessive αὐτοῦ. For the Ethiopian, it is no longer the road from Jerusalem to Gaza, descending toward the seacoast. Neither is it the road going back to his country. It is his road, it belongs to him, as a part of him. His road, that is his life, is now a life made of joy (χαίρων). Another occurrence is also important: ὁδηγήσει με (v. 31).[20] Actually, the Ethiopian asks for somebody to lead him, literally 'to road him'. Though on the road leading him back home, he was lost, in the middle of the desert, with no compass.

Patterns

Why was the Ethiopian lost? Two sound patterns provide the answer. The first one is based on Isaiah 53:7: 'He did not open his mouth' (οὕτως οὐκ ἀνοίγει τὸ στόμα αὐτοῦ), repeated in a modified pattern (v. 35): 'Then Philip opened his mouth' (ἀνοίξας δὲ ὁ Φίλιππος τὸ στόμα αὐτοῦ). The text read by the Ethiopian is far from being positive and encouraging. A sheep slaughtered, a lamb silent, with his mouth shut, a humiliating situation with no access to justice, a generation with no future on earth. Nothing to rejoice about indeed. In addition, the Ethiopian's reading is meaningless as it points to a mysterious and hidden character. But this first pattern includes an itinerary: it moves from closure to

---

19 Cf. Margaret Lee and Bernard Brandon Scott, *Sound Mapping the New Testament* (Salem: Polebridge, 2009), 135-166. See chapter four on repetitions.
20 See also Acts 2:28 and 9:2.

disclosure. The desert of the Ethiopian with no voice is transformed into a place where somebody opens his mouth: Philip.

The second pattern points to the sounds of the dialogue between Philip and the Ethiopian (vv. 30-32). It is based on specific techniques. First, alliterations (repetition of initial sounds). The verb γινώσκω is repeated three times in the expanded form ἀναγινώσκοντος/ ἀναγινώσκεις/ἀνεγίνωσκεν. Second, homoioteleuton (repetition of final sounds): γινώσκεις/ἀναγινώσκεις. Those three verses, at the very centre of the pericope, highlight the issue at stake: ἀνεγίνωσκεν and γίνωσκεν. Reading and understanding.

Thematic Sounds

'By assigning priority to certain sounds, repetition serves as a primary tool for guiding interpretation.'[21] Two sounds are repeated in this pericope: first, the preposition ἀνά (above). It features four times:

- v. 26: ἀνάστηθι (get up)
- v. 27: ἀναστὰς (having got up)
- v. 31: ἀναβάντα (Philip ran up)
- v. 39: ἀνέβησαν (they came up)
- Second, the preposition κατά, in contraposition to ἀνά. It occurs three times:
- v. 26: καταβαίνουσαν (the road that goes down)
- v. 36: κατὰ τὴν ὁδόν (they were going down the road)
- v. 38: κατέβησαν (both of them went down in the water)

The last occurrence is significant. The technique of homoioteleuton is used once again in the opposition κατέβησαν/ ἀνέβησαν (v. 38). At the beginning of the pericope, the Ethiopian was going down from Jerusalem. The audience is not told what his experience in the city was. Usually, pilgrims are described on their way up to the temple. Full of joy, they sang songs of ascent. The Bible never tells stories of pilgrims on their way back home. The only thing we know regarding the Ethiopian is his descent into the desert, during which he is still in a

---

21 Lee, *Sound Mapping the New Testament*, 151.

religious disposition, reading and searching in vain for meaning. But his descent is not ad inferno. He went up, not only out of the baptismal pool, but up into life, full of joy.²² Located at the end of the narrative, the opposition κατέβησαν/ ἀνέβησαν provides a clue for the interpretation of Isaiah's quotation. Abasement and raising are the two inseparable sides of the Christian coin. The servant of the Lord experienced both. The good news proclaimed by Philip concerns Jesus, raised from humiliation. In his baptism, the Ethiopian eunuch experiences like his Saviour the passage from humiliation to life.

Characterisation

Philip

Philip's role in the Ethiopian's narrative can only be rightly understood provided the reader enlarges their perspective. What is said of Philip before this episode is as important as what is said in this story. Philip is one of the seven men belonging to the group of Hellenists, chosen to share the food fairly in the daily distribution. The Hellenists were Jews, probably coming from the Diaspora, whose mother tongue was Greek and not Aramaic. Bestowed with wisdom and with the Spirit, being of good standing in the congregation, their work was to wait at table. Their help in household tasks would allow the apostles to concentrate on serving the Word.²³

Surprisingly, the book of Acts does not tell how this appointment came into practice. In a summary, it describes instead how 'the word of God continued to spread greatly in Jerusalem, especially among the priests' ,²⁴ not because of the apostles' work but thanks to Stephen's initiatives. But whereas Stephen's mission field was Jerusalem and the council, Philip's territory extends to Samaria. The man in charge of waiting at table, who never did so, is now serving the Word

---

22   See the difference with the ruler who became sad after having heard Jesus' words (Luke 19:23).
23   Cf. Acts 6:1-6.
24   Cf. Acts 6:7.

outside of the limited and exclusive territory of Israel, going far beyond his call of duty, which is a significant trait of his characterisation.

Second, Philip is directly connected to the divine.[25] There is no trace of him discussing the divine orders, nor any trace of delay in their execution. He is told to get up and to go: he got up and went (Acts 8:26). He is told to go over to the chariot and join it: better than going over to it, he ran up to it (Acts 8:30). A passive instrument in the hands of the divine, Philip is snatched away and transported in a flash to Azotus (Ashdod), about 30 miles away.

Third and foremost, when he asks the Ethiopian whether he understands what he reads, Philip raises the hermeneutical question of understanding. Indeed, there are snatches of texts in the Synoptic Gospels where the question of understanding is suggested. But generally speaking, the dominant thought is that it is misunderstanding which prevails.[26] The hermeneutical endeavour initiated by Philip is articulated around the following phases: a) Meeting the Ethiopian where he stands. First, it means joining him on his chariot. Second, joining him in his reading, precisely in the book of Isaiah, and even more precisely in chapter 53. b) Hearing what is read and identifying what is read. This supposes a biblical knowledge above the average. c) Interpreting the text. Interpreting means going beyond the simple reading of the text. This includes providing an answer to the Ethiopian's question: 'who is he?' This includes an unveiling, the identification of the character behind Isaiah's quotation.[27] Interpretation also includes amplification because the word of God cannot be limited to one single text.

---

25 I prefer the generic term 'the divine' which permits us to take into consideration Luke's variations in his terminology, going from Ἄγγελος κυρίου (v. 26) to τὸ πνεῦμα (v. 29) and finally to πνεῦμα κυρίου (v. 39).

26 See for example Mark 9:30-32 where the disciples do not understand Jesus' words concerning his death. Matt 17:22-23 rewords Mark's account: the disciples are greatly distressed. See also Matt 16:5-12 and the disciples' misunderstanding regarding the yeast of the Pharisees. As for the disciples on the road to Emmaus (Luke 24), their situation is twofold: they do not believe in Jesus' resurrection. But Jesus' response is to open their minds to understand the scriptures. Same idea in Paul. See 2 Cor 3:7-18 where a veil prevents understanding.

27 Commentators discuss the quotation of Isaiah and note that in quoting LXX Isa 53: 7b-8c, Luke omits seemingly obvious references to the expiatory death of the servant of the Lord. Cf. for example Pervo, *Acts*, 225. See also Daniel Marguerat, *Les Actes des apôtres* (1-12), 309.

Hermeneutics always includes a journey, a 'from here to there'. d) Interpreting means finally reaching a goal, which is proclaiming the good news about Jesus.

The Ethiopian

For the first conversion of an individual in the book of Acts, one would have expected Luke to give him a name. This is not the case. This does not mean that the audience is left in limbo. On the contrary, details abound, which provide quite a sophisticated image of what is obviously the main character in the narrative. At the end of the pericope, the portrait drawn by Luke is by far the most precise ever given in Acts.

ἰδοὺ ἀνὴρ

The first indication is so unusual that most translations skip it. Not followed by a genitive which would have pointed to a wife and impose the meaning of husband, ἀνήρ can only be taken as a gender indicator. The character is a male, not a female.

Αἰθίοψ

The second indicator is also unusual. The word Αἰθίοψ only features in Acts 8 in the NT. The OT uses the word 'כושׁ (Kushi/Kushites) to name the residents of Ethiopia.[28] In this grammatical construction, the word should be understood according to its etymology. Αἰθίοψ means a sun-burnt face, a clear indication that the male is black. This is not only a reference to skin colour. In those times, black people were often associated with immoral behaviour, and with demons.[29]

εὐνοῦχος

The word εὐνοῦχος comes in contraposition to ἀνὴρ and makes the gender identity of the black man complex. As put by Kartzow, 'their [εὐνοῦχος] gender status

---

28 This roughly corresponds today to the Northern part of Sudan.
29 Kartzow, 'Complex Identities: Ethnicity, Gender and Religion in the Story of the Ethiopian Eunuch (Acts 8:26-40),' *Religion and Theology*, 17 (2010): 192.

made them deviant from normal masculine behaviour'.³⁰ According to Lucian, 'a eunuch was neither man nor woman, but something composite, hybrid, and monstrous, alien to human nature'.³¹ Eunuchs bore the stigma of a complex gender identity.³² Their status was ambiguous.³³ In the Mediterranean world, the socio-religious opinion was sharply antagonistic to them.³⁴ Nonetheless, opposite views regarding their status ran through the OT, from strong rejection including exclusion from the assembly of the Lord (Deut 23:1), to Isaiah including the eunuchs into sabbath-keeping and covenant (56: 3-7).

δυνάστης Κανδάκης βασιλίσσης Αἰθιόπων

Whereas the word Αἰθίοψ (v. 27a) was a reference to race, in this second part of the verse it refers first to geography: the eunuch is a citizen of the kingdom of Ethiopia. Ethiopia was not part of the Roman empire. It represented the south, the far end of the world, but also the enemy always resisting imperial rule. Second, it indicates his status as a member of the royal court (δυνάστης ἐπὶ πάσης τῆς γάζης αὐτῆς), the queen's chancellor³⁵ of the exchequer in charge of finances.

ἐληλύθει προσκυνήσων εἰς Ἰερουσαλήμ ... ὑποστρέφων

This important detail regarding the Ethiopian often raises incorrect interpretations. The question is not the religious status of the eunuch, whether he was a φοβούμενος τὸν θεὸν or a proselyte, or whether he was able to enter the temple or not despite his otherness as a eunuch. The temple is clearly absent from this

---

30   Kartzow, 'Complex Identities: Ethnicity, Gender and Religion in the Story of the Ethiopian Eunuch (Acts 8:26-40)', 194.
31   Lucian of Samosata, *The Eunuch* 6 (Loeb Classical Library; Cambridge: Harvard University Press, 1913).
32   The issue of castration is widely discussed by commentators. See Annette Weissenrieder who considers that hemocromatisis could explain the eunuch's physiological situation. Annette Weissenrieder, 'Searching for the Middle Ground from the End of the Earth; The Embodiment of Space in Acts 8:26-40)', *Neotestamentica* 48 (2014): 135-36.
33   Anna Rebecca Solevåg, 'No Nuts? No Problem! Disability, Stigma, and the Baptized Eunuch in Acts 8:26-40', *Biblical Interpretation* 24 (2016): 89-90.
34   Kartzow, 'Complex Identities: Ethnicity, Gender and Religion in the Story of the Ethiopian Eunuch (Acts 8:26-40)', 193, 199.
35   The historian Strabo describes that this queen is 'a masculine sort of woman'. See Kartzow, 'Complex Identities: Ethnicity, Gender and Religion in the Story of the Ethiopian Eunuch (Acts 8:26-40)', 196.

account. There is no reason to introduce it into the text. The most important element in the characterisation is that the eunuch is returning from his journey to Jerusalem. The least that can be said is that, as he is on his way back, descending from Jerusalem, he is presented as an abnormal pilgrim. One may wonder if a returning pilgrim is still a pilgrim. Nothing is said regarding his time in the city. Specifically, this verse points to the relocation of sacred space. The first place of the relocation is the intermediary desert, the well-known place of God's revelation.

ἀνεγίνωσκεν

The verb ἀναγινώσκω is mainly used by Jesus, in the aorist form of ἀνέγνωτε ('have you not read').[36] This may sound as a rebuke: 'you should have read, but you did not.' This is not the case in this pericope. The eunuch reads, eagerly. One cannot ignore that this reading includes a high price and probably some challenges to overcome.[37] There were no online providers in Jerusalem, nor any religious bookshops open for foreign eunuchs. In his chariot driven by his servants, tossed about on the bumpy desert road, not waiting to be comfortably settled back home, the eunuch cannot wait to discover more about his burgeoning faith.

τις ὁδηγήσει με;

In his katabasis on the desert road, the Ethiopian is like a blind traveller.[38] However, instead of stubbornness, he shows humility and asks for help. He acknowledges that there is something in the text to which he could not have direct access, except via an interpreter.

---

36   Cf. Matt 12:3, 5; 19:4: 21:16, 42; 22:31; Mark 2:25; 12:10, 26; Luke 6:3.
37   Estimates for a 66-chapter long scroll of Isaiah (papyrus+scribal work) could reach hundreds of pounds or euros. Moreover, it is not certain that many scribes were ready to supply a non-Jew with such a copy of 'sacred' scripture.
38   Weissenrieder, 'Searching for the Middle Ground from the End of the Earth; The Embodiment of Space in Acts 8:26-40)', 145.

ἀποκριθεὶς δὲ ὁ εὐνοῦχος

The reading resonates. But the reading remains obscure and arcane. Commentators often misread the verb ἀποκρίνομαι. It does not mean 'to ask', but 'to answer', 'to reply'.[39] Despite his quite limited grasp of the text, the Ethiopian enters into a dialogue with it, questioning it with no passive submission to its abstruseness.

χαίρων

Luke uses the verb χαίρω nineteen times.[40] In his gospel, he dedicates a whole chapter (Luke 15) to remind the readership how joy is core to the good news of Jesus. In the introduction to this three-part parable, the key to understanding is provided: this is a response to the grumbling Pharisees, accusing Jesus because he welcomes sinners and eats with them.

The opening of the gospel to Samaria had caused concern among the Jerusalem authorities, who sent Peter and John to monitor the situation. Paul is already on his way to Damascus, driven by his evil plan, not knowing that the Lord is waiting for him on the way. The doors had to be wide open before he could begin his evangelical wanderings. The conversion of the eunuch unlocks all the locks. That of gender, including ambiguous gender, that of skin colour, that of geographical origin,[41] also in a nutshell that of circumcision as an identity marker. A castrated male is welcome in the community of believers. Soon, non-circumcised men will also be accepted.[42]

---

39   See Mark 11:14 where Jesus 'responds' to the fig tree!
40   Only two times with the current meaning of greeting. See Acts 15:23 and 23:26.
41   Weissenrieder, 'Searching for the Middle Ground from the End of the Earth; The Embodiment of Space in Acts 8:26-40'. 122.
42   Selovåg, 'No Nuts? No Problem! Disability, Stigma, and the Baptized Eunuch in Acts 8:26-40' 94.

Pervo is right when he claims that this pericope contains 'Lukan theology in a nutshell'.[43] But there is something more attached to it: it also provides a biblical paradigm for hermeneutics.

A Biblical Paradigm for Hermeneutics

Hermeneutics is a complex and demanding field of study. Applied to biblical sciences and theology, this domain of knowledge is in a paradoxical situation for the following reasons. First, there is overall a decline in general biblical knowledge. The Bible societies are selling more and more Bibles, but in theological faculties and seminaries, teachers are generally frightened by the biblical illiteracy of the students. Second, exegetical tools are now available to most people, whether in written or electronic form. Accessing the meaning of ancient texts is no longer an insurmountable task. Third, fundamentalist and biblicist currents are on the rise. For them, what the Bible says God says, and there is no need for interpretation, which is even considered as dangerous. Fourth, there is a decline in the teaching of philosophy. Since hermeneutics presupposes at least a basic knowledge in this field, few students are sufficiently equipped. Finally, anti-intellectualism is rampant in some quarters, under the guise of a biased understanding of the universal priesthood: anyone can understand and interpret. In sum, for too many readers and unfortunately some exegetes, it is as if verses 31 to 40 should be cut out. The story would then be of an Ethiopian reading Isaiah on his chariot. And the message would be straightforward: Imitate the Ethiopian. Read the Bible, brothers and sisters! Please read!

This castration of the text to parallel the castration of the eunuch is unacceptable, not only for the sake of the text itself, but also for the sake of reason. Instead, we propose a biblical paradigm for interpretation which is deployed in different phases.

---

43   Pervo, *Acts*, 66.

Phase 1: The Text

In the previous century, it would have been unacceptable to start building a paradigm without putting the author of a text at the front. This led to outstanding commentaries of the Bible, and excellent monographs where talented scholars showed their universal knowledge, their ability like Scotland Yard agents to find the slightest clue to identify the culprit, in this case, the biblical author always hidden behind a bush. But in too many cases, the historical-critical method only provided either different possible identifications of the author, or unsolved enigma, which prevented a final indisputable judgement.

Obviously, it is the text of Isaiah which is at the centre of the Ethiopian narrative. No text, no reader. No text, no hermeneutist to explain it. No text, no unveiling development leading to Christ. The text is the founding block of the narrative. What is its status, or in other words, what is a text?

From the narrative itself, the text does not fall from heaven into the hands of the reader. First, even though nothing is said on this matter, the text is to be searched, and paid for. Second, the text is not a relic brought back home by the Ethiopian to show off in his personal library or in a museum. The text is a text provided it is read and only if it is read. In other words, in itself the text is not magical, with an intrinsic power. Its power comes from outside. Moreover, the text raises questions and leaves them unanswered. It does not say to whose character Isaiah is pointing. Therefore, the text is insufficient. Its meaning should come from elsewhere. Though massive and solid like a rock, by nature a text is mute, and arcane.

To penetrate the block, different approaches have developed from the last century on. Among the main contributions, one cannot ignore Ferdinand de Saussure (1857-1913), the Swiss linguist and founder of modern linguistics.[44] His key concept of synchrony versus diachrony has made a significant impact on the study of texts. From a different perspective, Vladimir Propp highlighted homogenous and repeated structures in narratives.[45] Among the seven spheres of action he proposed, it would not be difficult to identify in the narrative the

---

44 Cf. Ferdinand de Saussure, *Cours de linguistique générale* (Genève, 1916), only translated into English in 1959: Course in General Linguistics (New York: Columbia University Press, 1959).
45 Cf. Vladimir Propp, *A Morphology of the Folktale* (Austin: University of Texas, 1968).

donor as the Holy Spirit, the helper as Philip, the hero as the Ethiopian. As for Philip's endeavour to use the scriptures to explain the quotation from Isaiah, it can be best understood in light of Julia Kristeva's contribution on intertextuality.[46] Even post-structural approaches, often challenging to say the least, may shed valuable light on texts. Jacques Derrida asserts the following:

> The question of the text ... has been transformed in the last dozen or so years. A text is no longer a finished corpus of writing, some content enclosed in a book or its margins, but a differential network, a fabric of traces, referring endlessly to something other than itself, to other differential sources.[47]

To sum up, according to Roland Barthes, 'the Text must not be thought of as a defined object.... The Text is a methodological field.... The Text is experienced only as an activity, a production.'[48] Who then would be in charge of this activity and production?

Phase 2: The Reader

The characterisation of the Ethiopian is so detailed and precise that the importance of the reader does not need further demonstration. As noted by Weissenrieder, 'The Ethiopian eunuch acts and speaks (v. 30 reading; v. 31 answering;[49] v. 34 saying; v. 36 exclaiming) and he understands: he sees the water (v. 36) and he descends into the water (v. 38). The text does not indicate that he is an object.'[50] The subject reader has to make a choice. It is their own decision to read, which implies getting access to the text via a manuscript, and the ability to read, on their own or via the use of a personal reader.[51] The subject reader decides to enter into a dialogue with the text, in which it does not play a dominant or

---

46   Cf. Julia Kristeva, *Revolution in Poetic Language* (New York: Columbia University Press, 1984).
47   Jacques Derrida, *Deconstruction and Criticism* (London: Continuum, 1995), 84.
48   Roland Barthes, *The Rustle of Language* (Berkeley: University of California, 1986). Cf. the chapter From Work to Text, 56-64.
49   Rather questioning. See above the meaning of ἀποκριθεὶς δὲ ὁ εὐνοῦχος.
50   Weissenrieder, 'Searching for the Middle Ground from the End of the Earth; The Embodiment of Space in Acts 8:26-40)', 139.
51   In the case of the Ethiopian, one can imagine that he had a servant/slave next to him in his chariot, in charge of reading aloud.

coercible role. The text is not covered with a halo of sanctity which would make it untouchable, and unapproachable. In the case of the Ethiopian, after having heard Isaiah 53, he questions the text: 'Who are you talking about? Of yourself or of somebody else?' In other words, the reader underlines the limits of the text, which does not contain clear clues to the identification of the character. In so doing, the reader also acknowledges his own limits. As a reader, he is not competent in his search for understanding. He needs a helper to lead him on his interpretation journey. A good subject reader is in essence a humble and flexible reader. The help of an external interpreter is all the more necessary as there are two categories of texts: open texts and closed texts. Closed texts are prescriptive, and their level of interpretation is limited. Open texts are descriptive, and their interpretation may be diverse.[52]

In short, the conclusion of the act of reading by the reading subject is not initially positive. This phase underlines the incompetence of the reader in search of meaning. It also highlights the limitations of the text as a tool leading directly to understanding. This reader phase should lead to the intervention of a third party. But the narrative also tells another story regarding the reader. The Ethiopian reader is a paragon of otherness. One would have expected as ideal reader a Jew, from the tribe of Judah, a son of Abraham, or better a γραμματεύς. No. Not a Jew, just a returning pilgrim, a black man, from the far end of the world, with an ambiguous gender and sexual identity! There is no prerequisite to Bible reading. All readers are welcome, whatever their gender, their race, their social rank, their sexual orientation. All readers are welcome, even though, like the Ethiopian eunuch, they cannot tick every box of the so-called 'normality' questionnaire.

Phase 3: The Meeting

At this point, the Lucan narrative has presented us with a text, and a reader. The text is mysterious and enigmatic. The reader is at a loss, for even if he has caught glimpses of it-he has understood that the text speaks of an important character-he is unable to identify him. In fact, the reader is at a dead end, suffering from

---

52   The book of Leviticus is clearly a closed text. The Sermon on the Mount as well. The apocalyptic literature is made of open texts. The hagiographs as well. Generally speaking, while the *halakah* is rather prescriptive (close text) the *haggadah* is descriptive (open text).

an unfulfilled quest for meaning. The encounter will transform this cul-de-sac into a path of life and joy.

The place of the meeting is important. The meeting could have happened in Jerusalem. It would have made sense for the Ethiopian who went there to worship God. Better, it could have happened in the Temple, or in a synagogue, the appropriate locations for this kind of encounter. But the place of the encounter is the place where the Ethiopian is, on his way back. He is not summoned by God or his messenger to a place of their choice. His geographical positioning on the road to Gaza is the place of encounter. That this place is in the desert is not neutral. It is obviously the privileged location for God's revelation.

The identity and function of Philip, the third party, are striking. Not only is he asked, after his successful missionary trip to Samaria, to go once more beyond the call of duty, but his Hellenistic roots give pause for thought. As a Hellenistic Jew, he is used to intercultural exchanges. He is familiar with Greek artifacts, practices, and modes of understanding.[53] In other words, he particularly qualifies to meet a stranger from the other side of the world.

The meeting is a three-voice dialogue. The first voice is that of Isaiah. In itself, this voice is silent. It is present in the text, but it cannot say anything more than what is written. It is precisely this silence that causes a problem, as it leaves the reader unsatisfied. The second voice is that of the Ethiopian. It is initially demanding, requesting help. It is then reactive, responding to the text (ἀποκριθείς). Finally, it demands once again: 'What is to prevent me from being baptised?' The third voice, that of Philip, is explanatory. Umberto Eco provides us here with an illuminating explanation of what is happening in the act of reading. He first considers that a text can be compared with a lazy machine. It requests the reader to do eager and cooperative work. More precisely, 'the text is a fabric woven of white spaces, interstices to be filled, and the one who wrote it has planned that those interstices would be filled and not left white'.[54] It implies that the reader is invited to participate in the production of the text, because

---

53   Cf. Robert A. Kugler, 'Hellenism, Hellenization,' *EDEJ*, ed. by John J. Collins and Daniel C. Harlow (Grand Rapids: Eerdmans, 2010): 723.
54   Cf. Umberto Eco, *Lector in Fabula* (Paris: Grasset, 1985). 63. Original version in Italian, 1979. The translation of Eco's books into English is challenging when compared to the original Italian texts. Chapters are sometimes reorganised. We quote from the French translation which seems in this respect to be more faithful to the Italian text.

it does not contain a meaning in itself. The contribution of the third voice is therefore revelatory. It includes the unveiling of the text, by which the gaps and interstices are filled. In this phase, the third voice helps the reader in a process of double fusion: the fusion of his personal horizon with the horizon of the text. In the case of the Ethiopian, the horizon of his humiliation as an ambiguous character merges with the horizon of the text which presents a suffering character who also experienced humiliation until he overcomes it.[55] In this unveiling deployment, the third voice does not operate freely, with no constraints.[56] The interpretation provided takes into consideration the horizon of the author, even though it may be difficult to access it, because it may be blurred by differing times and circumstances. Moreover, the proposed interpretation cannot ignore the other texts belonging to the same corpus–Scripture–nor previous interpretations. But at the same time, it cannot be bound by them. It means that the interpretation process cannot be repetitive. To understand is to understand something else.

In the beginning, there are words on a papyrus or a leather scroll. Sounds difficult to decipher. A dead end with no possible identification. Then a dialogue, including a helper, the hermeneutist. The veil is lifted. The unidentified is given a name. The mysterious text is put into a larger perspective. It leads to Christ. The mysterious and silent words become the Word of God. The process ends up in the reader act: baptism. There is no longer a dead end, but life with joy.

Conclusion

What does it mean to understand? Various and differing answers have been given to this question. Often sophisticated, sometimes illuminating, sometimes challenging, sometimes unacceptable. Different voices produce a cacophony from which it is difficult to find leading sound principles for interpretation.

The Ethiopian narrative places signposts along the hermeneutical path that deserve to be taken into consideration. Assuredly, the text is the cornerstone

---

55 Cf. Hans Georg Gadamer, *Truth and Method* (London: Bloomsbury, 1975), 301ff.

56 Another understanding of reader-response hermeneutics considers that there should not be a third voice, monitoring the interpretation. Per se, there is no fusion of the horizon of the reader with the horizon of the text. The horizon of the reader is in control of the interpretation.

of the hermeneutic endeavour. But the text is only an object. As Yvan Elissalde puts it, 'the love of the texts without the presence of somebody else is a business with the dead'.[57] On his chariot, the Ethiopian read and re-read Isaiah. But he crashed into the wall of its abstruseness. If reading is necessary, and inescapable, it remains void if it is not accompanied. It therefore becomes clear that the role of the hermeneutist is crucial. Without Philip's intervention, the Ethiopian would be the most unhappy of men, in possession of a safe to which he did not have the key. Philip breaks the secret. He lifts the veil. He provides the answer to the nagging question: do you understand what you read? The text as an object is miraculously transformed, under the powerful guidance of the spirit/angel of the Lord. The Ethiopian questions it and responds to it. It has become a place of dialogue, a tool leading to an encounter with the mysterious figure, Christ. The scroll of Isaiah has then become the WORD of God.

Philip disappears. This is not yet the end of the journey for the Ethiopian. The hermeneutic endeavour is never completed. He must continue his path, toward Gaza. Where he is precisely, we are not told. But it is not difficult to understand that when the conversation ends, the chariot has come nearer to Gaza.

Gaza means 'treasury'. The man in charge of the queen's treasury is now closer than ever to the real treasury. Carry on, brother. Carry on!

---

57 Cf. Yvan Elissalde, *Critique de l'interprétation* (Paris : Vrin, 2002), 76. My translation.

Blessed is the church which encourages Bible reading

Blessed is the church which trains hermeneutists

Blessed is the church which understands that hermeneutics no longer takes place in Jerusalem, nor in the temple

Blessed is the church which notes that hermeneutics is not taken care of by pontificating γραμματεῖς

Blessed is the church which understands that hermeneutics is not a monologue but a dialogue

Blessed is the church which encourages the search for new meanings rather than mindless repetitions

Blessed is the church which understands that hermeneutics is not a system of beliefs, but an encounter with the incarnate Word of God.

What if God is Absent?
The Challenge of Incorporating Esther into a Biblical Theology

Laurence A. Turner

Introduction

The purpose of this brief study is to address the potential contribution of the book of Esther to biblical theology. This might appear to be a bold, even foolhardy, task. For Esther is a theological problem. Indeed, 'of all the books in the Bible, the book of Esther might seem least available for theological analysis'.[1] To be more precise, it is the Hebrew version of Esther, accepted by Jews and Protestants as canonical, that causes the problem. Esther also exists in two Greek versions. One of these, the Septuagint (LXX), is considered canonical in Roman Catholicism and Eastern Orthodoxy. The other is the so-called Alpha-Text (AT), extant in only four medieval manuscripts. The LXX is considerably longer than the AT, but both are overtly theistic, and include six 'Additions', in five of which God, religious practice and general piety are prominent. The AT also includes overtly religious material in its main text.[2] By contrast, in the Hebrew version neither the narrator nor the characters mention God, no religious activity by either Jew or Persian is recorded, and the pietistic 'Additions' of the Greek versions are absent. It is an apparently 'godless' text and forms the

---
1   Elizabeth Newman, 'Where in the World Is God?: On Finding the Divine in Esther,' *Review & Expositor* 118.2 (2021): 180.
2   For example, 'Haman went to his gods' (4:7) to learn the propitious time to attack the Jews.

basis for this present study. In what follows, when I discuss the absence of God, I am referring to this literary absence of God from the text of Esther, not making any claims about his non-existence in an ontological sense.

There have been basically two approaches in the history of interpretation to the theologically resistant Hebrew text. The first, followed by the majority, is to claim that God, theology, and religious practice may be found in Esther if one has the reading competence to discover them. For many, penetrating the apparently profane surface of Esther to discover the theological treasures within is an easy manoeuvre. For example, God has been found in the narrative's extraordinary number of coincidences,[3] stunning reversals of fortune,[4] alleged cultic allusions in miscellaneous narrative details,[5] the dialogue between Esther and Mordecai in 4:14-16,[6] theological implications drawn from intertextual connections,[7] acrostics spelling out the divine name, or typologies,[8] to mention just a few attempts. Limitations of space prohibit engagement with the approaches

---

[3] E.g. Jean Daniel Macchi, *Le livre d'Esther, Commentaire de l'ancien testament* XIV (Geneva: Labor et Fides, 2016), 116; Barry G. Webb, *Five Festal Garments: Christian Reflections on the Song of Songs, Ruth, Lamentations, Ecclesiastes and Esther*, New Studies in Biblical Theology (Leicester: InterVarsity Press, 2000), 121.

[4] E.g. Frederick W. Bush, *Ruth, Esther*, WBC 9, ed. David A. Hubbard, Glenn W. Barker and Ralph P. Martin (Dallas: Word Books, 1996), 325; *Beate Ego, Ester*, BKAT XXI (Göttingen: Vandenhoeck & Ruprecht, 2017), 54.

[5] E.g. Max Frederick Rogland, 'The Cult of Esther: Temple and Priestly Imagery in the Book of Esther', *JSOT* 44.1 (2019): 99-114; Yitzhak Berger, 'Mordechai and Flowing Myrrh: On the Presence of God in the Book of Esther', *Tradition: A Journal of Orthodox Jewish Thought* 49.3 (2016): 20-21.

[6] E.g. Harald-Martin Wahl, *Das Buch Esther, Übersetzung und Kommentar* (Berlin, Boston: De Gruyter, 2009), 120-22.

[7] Out of numerous examples I simply note here representative recent arguments for connections with Jacob-Esau: Petr Chalupa, 'Jakob und Esau im Esterbuch', *CV* 58.3 (2016): 315-21. Joseph: Gabriel F. Hornung, 'The Theological Import of MT Esther's Relationship to the Joseph Story', *CBQ* 82.4 (2020): 567-81. Hannah: Justin Jackson, 'Raised up from the Dust: An Exploration of Hannah's Reversal Motif in the Book of Esther as Evidence of Divine Sovereignty', *Themelios* 46.3 (2021): 546-61. Daniel: Gregory Ross Goswell, 'The Place of the Book of Esther in the Canon', *TJ* 37.2 (2016): 170.

[8] For detailed discussions of alleged acrostics and typology in Esther, see my previous studies 'Desperately Seeking YHWH: Finding God in Esther's "Acrostics"', in *Interested Readers: Essays on the Hebrew Bible in Honor of David J. A. Clines*, ed. James K. Aitken, Jeremy M. S. Clines, and Christl M. Maier (Atlanta, GA: Society of Biblical Literature, 2013), 183-93; 'Finding Christ in a Godless Text: The Book of Esther and Christian Typology', in *No One Better: Essays in Honour of Norman H. Young*, ed. Robert K. McIver and Kayle de Waal (New York: Peter Lang, 2016), 5-21.

just mentioned or with the bewildering number of further suggestions that claim God can be found in Esther, and in many cases fairly easily at that. However, every suggestion that God or theology is the obvious intention of this or that detail in the text is open to serious question. As Anne-Mareike Wetter says, 'Of all the books of the Hebrew Bible, the book of Esther presents the most consistently silent God. Indeed, silence in this book is so pervasive that it is not even mentioned.'[9] Further, one issue rarely even recognised is this: if, as many claim, God can be found so easily, what purpose is served by readers having to search for him in the first place? In particular, what theological purpose is served by such divine silence?

Gunnar Pedersen has given much thought to how biblical theology should be conceived and constructed around the Bible's 'common theological horizon'.[10] Esther's unique 'godless' form provides an interesting example for investigating how that biblical-theological unanimity is confirmed or problematised. To what extent does Esther join the biblical choir as it sings in unison and how far do we hear it as a distinctive solo voice contrasting with, yet nevertheless contributing to, the scriptural concert?

Consequently, I suggest in this study that consideration be given to the theological potential of Esther in the minority approach to the text, which explores the obvious: that God, religious practice, and theology as conventionally conceived, are absent. This is what makes the book unique in Scripture.[11] By too easily 'discovering' within Esther theological themes and affirmations commonplace in the OT, we minimise the significance of the book's distinctive contribution: God is absent. 'All attempts on the part of critics to circumvent

---

9 Anne-Mareike Wetter, 'Speaking from the Gaps: The Eloquent Silence of God in Esther', in *Reflections on the Silence of God: A Discussion with Marjo Korpel and Johannes de Moor*, ed. Bob Becking, OtSt 62 (Brill: Leiden, 2013), 153.

10 Gunnar Pedersen and Ján Barna, 'A Search for the Biblical Epistemic Horizon: Towards Meta-Hermeneutics', *Spes Christiana* 32.2 (2021): 33; see also 'Towards a Scripture-Based Theology', in *Ecclesia Reformata, Semper Reformanda*, ed. Jean-Claude Verrecchia (Bracknell, UK: Newbold Academic Press, 2016), 149-77; 'The Bible as 'Story': A Methodological Opportunity', in *Exploring the Frontiers of Faith: Festschrift in Honour of Dr. Jan Paulsen*, ed. Børge Schantz and Reinder Bruinsma (Lueneberg: Advent-Verlag, 2009), 237-45.

11 Some believe Song of Songs is equally 'godless'. However, Song 8:6 includes the compound word שַׁלְהֶבֶתְיָה. The final element יָה is taken by many as a contraction of the divine name יהוה and translated 'flame of Yahweh'. Others treat it as a superlative, and translate 'mighty flame', or similar.

the areligiosity of the book of Esther shortchange the most remarkable characteristic of the book.'[12] Rather, we should ask the question as framed by Samuel Wells, 'What does the church know that it would otherwise not know'[13] if God had been explicitly present in Esther? How might the answer to this question enrich our biblical-theological reflections? My purpose in this brief account is not to provide definitive answers to these questions but rather to indicate fruitful possibilities for reading Esther theologically.

The Theological Potential of God's Absence in Esther

There have been many suggestions for theological significance in God's absence from Esther. For example, that it is evidence of an extreme piety. Reverence for the divine name caused readers of the OT to stop pronouncing the name of God (הוהי) and to substitute 'Lord' (ינדא). Esther takes this one step further, it is argued, by omitting even this substitution.[14] However, this is an unlikely solution to the problem because the Jewish characters in Esther engage in no religious practice at all. If piety is the reason for God's absence, one might think that there would be ample evidence of characters' spiritual enthusiasm and emphasis on the transcendent. But there is none.

Others have argued that the strategy of Esther is to convey spiritual reality. Jewish life in the diaspora clearly required a reassessment of the theological framework in which the faithful operated. They were away from the land of promise, the city of David, the temple and its cult etc. Old traditions needed refracting through the lens of their new reality. To the Jews, living in such novel circumstances, God appeared to be absent, missing from their lives, and therefore he is omitted from the plot of Esther. Some contemporary preachers have found this perspective amenable to homiletical application. That is, twenty-first century believers frequently feel as if they are alone, without God. Thus, Esther

---

12   André LaCocque, *Esther Regina: A Bakhtinian Reading, Rethinking Theory* (Evanston, IL: Northwestern University Press, 2008), 62.
13   Samuel Wells, 'Esther', in *Esther and Daniel*, Brazos Theological Commentary on the Bible, ed. R. R. Reno et al. (Grand Rapids: Brazos Press, 2013), 10.
14   Friedrich Wilhelm Schultz, *The Book of Esther: Theologically and Homiletically Expounded*, trans. James Strong, repr., Eugene, OR: Wipf & Stock, 2007. (Charles Scribner, 1877), 16. Cf. Christoph Horwitz, 'Zur Theologie des Buches Esther', *LB* 3.1/2 (1998): 98-99.

speaks powerfully to them in this post-Christian world.[15] However, no character in Esther ever expresses such a feeling. Like the narrator they neither mention God's absence as a problem nor yearn for his presence. The divine simply has no literary role in the text.

Nevertheless, there are at least two approaches to the absence of God in Esther that merit further consideration as making potential contributions to an overall biblical theology. Like any other approach to understanding the uniqueness of Esther, there are counterarguments, but these are not as persuasive, in my opinion, as those arguments countering the alternative view that God is transparently present. The following two suggestions are illustrative only, indicating possible fruitful perspectives for moving beyond traditional pietistic and devotional understandings of the narrative that have predominated in conservative assessments of the biblical text. The first suggestion–giving more attention to the neglected theme of God's increasing disappearance from the narrative action of the OT–might appeal to those whose biblical theology utilises the storyline of the biblical narrative as its framework. The second could make a case for Esther moving into the biblical-theological mainstream by suggesting a reassessment of the characters in the narrative–not as idealistic exemplars of covenant faithfulness but rather the opposite–and that this narrative intent makes God's absence both understandable and theologically motivated.

The Trajectory of God's Absence in the OT

Worthy of consideration is the possibility that Esther contributes to a development in the OT, noted recently by several scholars, which sees God moving increasingly into the background as one moves through the OT. One of the first to argue this at length was Richard Elliott Friedman, who maintains that 'gradually through the course of the Hebrew Bible ... the deity appears less and less to humans, speaks less and less. Miracles, angels, and all other signs of divine

---

15 Paul Blackham, 'Two Conspiracies Uncovered,' *Allsouls.Org*, 8 July 2007, http://www.allsouls.org/Media/Player.aspx?media_id=49814&file_id=55159. Cf. Debra Reid, *Esther: An Introduction and Commentary*, *TOTC* 13 (Nottingham/Downers Grove, IL: Inter-Varsity Press/InterVarsity Press, 2008), 54.

presence become rarer and finally cease. In the last portions of the Hebrew Bible, God is not present in the well-known apparent ways of the earlier books'.[16]

For Friedman, the giving of the Decalogue is the high point of God's audio-visual communication with Israel, and also the last time he addresses the nation as a whole. From this point on 'the apparent presence of God in the Bible starts to diminish'.[17] Public miracles (as distinguished from private affairs for individuals or small groups) become rarer as one moves through Joshua to Judges, and this trend gains momentum so that by the time the reader reaches 2 Samuel there are almost no miracles at all. God 'reveals' himself to Samuel, but never again directly to any individual. The shekinah glory is last seen at the dedication of Solomon's temple.

After the contest between Elijah and the prophets of Baal on Mount Carmel (1 Kgs 18) there are no public miracles, claims Friedman, and then even private miracles cease after Hezekiah (2 Kgs 20:8-11). While the miracles of the book of Daniel might seem to be an exception to this, the people of Judah as a whole witness none of them. By the time we reach Ezra and Nehemiah, there are 'no miracles, no angels, no divine appearances. God is never said to have spoken to anyone.'[18] As God moves away from centre stage, human initiative and responsibility come to the fore.

Jack Miles's reading of God's characterisation in the Hebrew Bible comes to comparable conclusions, though his mode of reading is somewhat different. Whereas Friedman reads chronologically, that is, reading the biblical books not in the order in which they were written, nor in their canonical sequence, but in the order in which they track Israel's actual history, Miles reads in strict Hebrew canonical order from Genesis to Chronicles.[19]

In responding to these observations, I would note that while the biblical text does support the general trend of the distancing of God, at the same time it indicates a more complicated development than Friedman or Miles allow. For example, a similar phenomenon can be observed on a smaller scale in the book of Genesis as one traces the developments in divine characterisation and human

---

16   Richard Elliott Friedman, *The Disappearance of God* (New York: Little, Brown, 1995), 7.
17   Friedman, *Disappearance*, 16.
18   Friedman, *Disappearance*, 27.
19   See Jack Miles, *God: A Biography* (New York: Knopf, 1995).

responsibility.[20] As one moves from the beginning to the end of Genesis, God increasingly retreats to the background of the narrative, a fact confirmed not merely statistically[21] but also by the ways in which humanity assumes increasing responsibility for plot developments and adopts a more confident posture in speaking to or about God. Whereas the Man in the Garden replies to the Lord's questioning with a beguiling simplicity, 'The Woman whom you gave to be with me' (Gen 3:12), and never protests the consequences, his successors adopt a more robust stance. Abraham's questioning of God's justice (18:22-33) and Jacob's physically wrestling with one who is more than human (32:22-32), are examples of a maturing human confidence in the presence of God. By the time we meet Joseph, we encounter an individual operating in a narrative with few explicit mentions of God's presence. Rather, Joseph tends to speak on God's behalf. This development at the end of Genesis marks the inversion of the situation at the beginning of the book. The narrative has moved from the primeval history's picture of divine omnipresence and omnipotence in God's relationship with humanity to one in which humans are now centre-stage and God's involvement is conveyed almost exclusively via comments by characters and narrator only.[22]

This movement in Genesis bears comparison with that claimed by Friedman, Miles, and others for the OT as a whole.[23] However, the momentum beginning in Genesis peters out in Exodus. While the first two chapters of Exodus have much to say about the dilemma of Israel enslaved in Egypt, God's involvement is minimal. At the end of ch. 2, however, he makes up for lost time. He *hears* Israel's groaning; *remembers* his covenant with the patriarchs; *looks* upon his people;

---

20 See Robert L. Cohn, 'Narrative Structure and Canonical Perspective in Genesis', *JSOT* 25 (1983): 3-16. For further utilization of Cohn's basic insights see e.g. Laurence A. Turner, 'Genesis, Book of', in *Dictionary of the Old Testament: Pentateuch*, ed. T. Desmond Alexander and David W. Baker (Downers Grove, IL/ Leicester: Inter-Varsity Press, 2003), 352-56.

21 The terms יְהוָה and אֱלֹהִים occur a total of 129 times in the Primeval History; 97 in the Abraham story; 81 in the Jacob cycle; and 47 in the story of Jacob's Family.

22 Cohn, 'Narrative Structure,' 15. For a detailed discussion of related matters see Laurence A. Turner, *Announcements of Plot in Genesis* (Eugene, OR: Wipf and Stock, 2008), 143-73; Cf. W. Lee Humphreys, *The Character of God in the Book of Genesis: A Narrative Appraisal* (Louisville: Westminster John Knox Press, 2001).

23 See John Goldingay, *Old Testament Theology* (Downers Grove, IL/Milton Keynes: InterVarsity Press/Paternoster Press, 2003), 1: Israel's Gospel: 785-86.

and finally, and enigmatically, 'God *knew* (וַיֵּדַע)' (Exod 2:24-25). This initiates God's self-revelation to Moses in the wilderness of Midian, and his announcement that he will free Israel from bondage. That freedom is achieved through a series of divine signs and wonders that see God involved more directly and frequently than he has been since the events of the primeval history. In other words, while there is a general movement in the OT where God increasingly moves into the background, that trajectory is neither straight nor consistent.[24] Through the four main sections of Genesis, decreasing divine presence and increasing human initiative do follow an approximately straight line of development. If Genesis had a fifth and final section in which this trend continued, then the book would end with a narrative not that far removed from Esther, as far as God's presence is concerned. But, of course, such is not the case. Exodus marks a resumption of divine initiative such as that found in the early chapters of Genesis. Subsequently, as the OT continues, God's presence traverses peaks and troughs in its general descent towards divine absence, rather than in a consistent straight line. Consequently, the biblical text juxtaposes divine presence and absence during that journey. Nevertheless, as Sun states,

> the visibility and activity of God gradually diminishes as the biblical books progress to the end.... If we take the canon of the Hebrew Bible, with its tripartite division–the Torah, the Prophets, and the Writings—into consideration, the trajectory of a disappearing God emerges.[25]

Koller also observes,

> While the graph of divine involvement [in the Hebrew Bible] is not a straight line with a negative slope, ending at zero, it does clearly have a trendline, and that clearly does have a negative slope. Assuming Friedman's canonical reading has

---

24 Brittany Melton, in a significant and highly engaging monograph, is dismissive of Friedman's entire enterprise. She is correct in criticising his oversimplification of the movement of God's disappearance from the biblical text. I have pointed out some of these deficiencies in my assessment above. However, she dismisses too many of his insights too quickly, in my opinion. See Brittany N. Melton, *Where Is God in the Megilloth?: A Dialogue on the Ambiguity of Divine Presence and Absence*, Oudtestamentische Studiën 73 (Leiden; Boston: Brill, 2018), 15-19.
25 Chloe Sun, *Conspicuous in His Absence* (Downers Grove, IL: InterVarsity Press, 2021), 39-40.

methodological validity, there is a powerful and clear statement being made over the course of the Hebrew Bible about the changing (i.e. decreasing) role of God in the world.[26]

It is worth noting at this point how some OT texts juxtapose divine absence and presence. This is, of course, a frequently observed characteristic in the psalms of lament. There are abrupt shifts from God's perceived absence or indolence to praise for his presence and steadfast love (e.g. Ps 13:1-4, cf. vv. 5-6). In the same narrative genre as Esther, there are some similar movements. For example, Gideon responds to the angel of the Lord's salutation, 'The LORD is with you', by asking 'if the LORD is with us, why then has all this happened to us?' (Judg 6:12b-13a). However, Gideon's complaint about God's seeming absence soon shifts to an acknowledgement of God's presence, 'I have seen the angel of the LORD face to face', followed by the Lord's direct speech to him (Judg 6:22b-23).[27] Significantly, however, Esther does not conform to this narrative pattern. It is silent on divine absence and notes no instance of divine presence.[28]

Mark McEntire agrees with the basic observations above on the trajectory of God's characterisation and receding literary presence in the OT. In teasing out the biblical-theological implications, his most provocative suggestion is that the end of this story should move from the periphery to the centre of OT theology. If the characterisation of God has indeed developed from an all-powerful interventionist who speaks directly to humans and whose actions are unambiguous and frequently miraculous (e.g. creation, flood, exodus, conquest etc.), to Ezra-Nehemiah where, while God is referred to frequently by Ezra, Nehemiah and others, God does not speak or act directly, then there are theological implications. If the end of the OT story sees humans speaking to God (e.g. Ezr 9:10; Neh 13:31) but not vice versa, and any divine action is not overt but interpreted

---

26 Aaron Koller, in his review of Melton's book above. See https://www.sblcentral.org/API/Reviews/12454_13880.pdf.
27 See Joel S. Burnett, 'The Question of Divine Absence in Israelite and West Semitic Religion,' *CBQ* 67.2 (2005): 219; 'Where Is God?: Divine Absence in Israelite Religion,' *PRSt* 33.4 (2006): 404.
28 This fact alone demonstrates that Esther's inclusion in the Megilloth is not sufficient to explain God's absence. In Ecclesiastes, God occurs in 34 verses. 'The LORD' appears in 42 verses of Lamentations, and in Ruth 16 times. The LORD's presence in the text of Song of Songs, as noted, is disputed. However, if we accept its presence there, Esther is as distinct from the rest of the Megilloth on the absence of God as the Megilloth are from the rest of the OT in other areas.

as such by the narrator (e.g. Ezr 1:5; 5:5), or characters (e.g. Ezr 6:12; 7:27; Neh 2:8; 4:15), then perhaps we have arrived at the climax of the OT storyline. Such a trajectory 'would seem to point toward a narrative method of doing theology which gives this endpoint a place of privilege'.[29]

The challenge, as McEntire notes, is that biblical theology usually privileges the beginning rather than the end of the OT narrative progression. Volumes on OT theology habitually stress the beginning at the expense of the end.[30] However, if the end were moved towards the centre of the OT theological enterprise, Esther might cease being a theological liability. Esther's complete exclusion of explicit theological language is admittedly extreme, yet it sits more comfortably with other relatively neglected books at the end of the OT journey than it does with those at the outset of the journey. It might also raise some questions rarely asked yet potentially significant. For example, why do we have to wait to the end of the OT story to encounter a book that eliminates God altogether from its discourse? Why does such a strategy not occur before? And what might the implications of this be for an overall biblical theology? From a Christian perspective, how might this anticipate or complicate New Testament theology?

Finally, a significant methodological question to ponder:

> Do we look at the life of God in the Hebrew Scriptures all at once, seeking language which speaks of that whole life at the same time, or do we follow that life through narrative time, arriving at an articulation of the nature of God's character that has left some aspects behind and arrived at a particular identity?[31]

---

[29] Mark McEntire, 'The God at the End of the Story: Are Biblical Theology and Narrative Character Development Compatible?', *HBT* 33.2 (2011): 171.

[30] As McEntire notes, 'In Brueggemann's *Theology* references to Genesis alone outnumber references to all of Chronicles, Ezra, and Nehemiah together by a ratio of 3 to 1, and the scripture index of James Barr's *Concept of Biblical Theology* contains not a single reference to Chronicles, Ezra, or Nehemiah. Esther finds no place in either book. The field of theology of the Hebrew Scriptures has always had more interest in the earlier part of the narrative about God than in its conclusion.' McEntire, 'The God at the End of the Story', 186.

[31] McEntire, 'The God at the End of the Story', 189.

God's Absence as Evidence of His Judgement

Another possibility for theological reflection on God's absence from Esther, is to reassess the role and characterisation of its Jewish characters. Rather than being paragons of virtue and Jewish faithfulness, are they depicted as being non-observant covenant-breakers? If so, God's absence could be evidence of his judgement. While biblical narrators sometimes provide explicit judgement of characters' failures (e.g. 2 Sam 12:1-12; 1 Kgs 16:30), more frequently they do not, leaving such assessments to their readers. So, in principle, it is at least feasible that readers should assess Esther, Mordecai and the Jews negatively, even in the absence of a specific narrative condemnation. After all, not only are there pervasive biblical traditions that Judah was exiled as punishment for its covenant infidelity (e.g. Jer 7:12-15; cf. Josh 23:16; Deut 31:16-18), but in Esther the Jews–Esther and Mordecai included–seemingly display covenant non-observance.

The provenance of the book can have some bearing on how it might be interpreted from this perspective. Most see it as the product of the diaspora, reflecting what life was like for those beyond the border of the promised land. Others take issue with this. For example, Stern argues that it was written in Judea as an anti-diasporic text. Its aim is to undermine the type of Judaism practised in the diaspora and this goes some way towards explaining the hyperbolic and farcical form of the narrative. The narrative's exaggeration is the vehicle for its 'comic critique' of a lifestyle that abandons what its writer considered normative for Judaism–faithfulness to God, adherence to the Jerusalem cult, observance of mosaic festivals etc.[32]

In comparable fashion, Pierce argues that the contrast between the non-observance of the covenant by the Jews on the one hand, and 'God's steadfast grace and providential care for his people'[33] on the other, establishes a strong basis for a theological interpretation of the book. That is, the faithlessness of the

---

32 Elsie R. Stern, 'Esther and the Politics of Diaspora', *JQR* 100.1 (2010): 25-53.
33 Ronald W. Pierce, 'The Politics of Esther and Mordecai: Courage or Compromise?', *BBR* 2 (1992): 82. See also Louis A. Brighton, 'The Book of Esther–Textual and Canonical Considerations', *Concordia Journal* 13 (1987): 211.

characters plays a subsidiary role to the overarching theological intention, which is to counter that vice.[34]

Dunne spells out the failings of the Jews in detail. He claims that the Jews' behaviour reveals their lack of covenant commitment and their assimilation into Persian culture. They choose to remain in Persia decades after they could have returned to Jerusalem, their home city (2:6). They do not celebrate the Passover, even when the narrative's chronology overlaps with the time of its observance.[35] The book's persistence in naming the female protagonist by her Persian name 'Esther', rather than her Jewish one 'Hadassah', underlines the Jews' preferred Persian identity. In short, there are no explicit references in the book to Jewish observance of the covenant. It is not simply that the book fails to mention such details but rather that it provides evidence of active covenant unfaithfulness. To the points above we might add others, such as Esther's marriage to an uncircumcised foreign king. However, perhaps most telling is Mordecai's instruction to Esther when she entered the royal court that she should not reveal to anyone that she was a Jew (2:10), which she dutifully obeyed (2:19). If Esther were religiously observant, that would be impossible.

Dunne and others also criticise Mordecai and Esther for serious moral failings. For example, they take plunder from the Agagite Haman (8:1-2), thus repeating the sin of their ancestor King Saul (2:5; cf. 1 Sam 15:8-9). Also, Esther's retribution is excessive and vindictive (e.g. 9:5-17), showing that the persecuted

---

34 Scott M. Langston, 'Reading a Text Backwards: The Book of Esther and Nineteenth-Century Jewish American Interpretations', in *The Book of Esther in Modern Research*, ed. Sidnie White Crawford and Leonard J. Greenspoon, JSOTSup 380 (London: T & T Clark International, 2003), 202.
35 Haman's decree was published on 13 Nisan (3:12-13), and Esther's fasting lasted until 15 Nisan (4:15), thus replacing the celebration of Passover with a fast. See e.g. Jürg Hutzli, '"Ištar" und "Marduk" als jüdische Protagonisten, Purim als neues Fest der Befreiung: Zur Theologie und zum historischen Ort des Esterbuches', *VT* 72.2 (2022): 13; Jean Daniel Macchi, 'Dieu, la Perse et le courage d'être juive: réflexions sur Esther 4', *FoiVie* 103.4 (2004): 73; Le livre d'Esther, 119.

have themselves become persecutors.³⁶ However, such allegations of wholesale moral depravity have been seriously questioned, and with some justification.³⁷

The charges of general Jewish covenant unfaithfulness, however, are not so easily discounted. After all, the reason they are in Persia rather than in Judah is the consequence of God's previous judgement. Reading the book in its larger canonical context finds one inter-text in particular which encourages reading Esther as an account of covenant unfaithfulness. Deuteronomy 31:18 states, 'On that day I will surely hide (הַסְתֵּר אַסְתִּיר) my face on account of all the evil they have done by turning to other gods.' As Beal notes,³⁸ broad connections to Esther have been drawn from this text from early rabbinic times. More specifically, God's emphatic assertion, 'I shall surely hide', is expressed using two causative (hiphil) forms of סתר, infinitive absolute and imperfect. Esther's unvocalised name (אסתר)³⁹ could be read as identical in meaning to the imperfect (אסתיר) in Deut 31:18, that is, 'I will hide', which has encouraged reflections on possible significance. Esther's name could be interpreted positively as an affirmation of providence. That is, God is working behind the scenes in hidden ways for the salvation of his people. However, this suggestion concerning the hiding of the 'face of God' does not do justice to the idiomatic use of the

---

36   See John Anthony Dunne, *Esther and Her Elusive God: How a Secular Story Functions as Scripture* (Eugene, OR: Wipf & Stock, 2014), 15-67; Cf. Pierce, 'Politics', 82-87; F. B. Huey Jr, 'Irony as the Key to Understanding the Book of Esther', *SwJT* 32 (1990): 37-39; Marjo C. A. Korpel, 'Theodicy in the Book of Esther', in *Theodicy in the World of the Bible*, ed. Antii Laato and Johannes C. De Moor (Leiden/Boston: Brill, 2003), 352-58.

37   See e.g. Marvin A. Sweeney, 'Absence of G-d and Human Responsibility in the Book of Esther', in *Reading the Hebrew Bible for a New Millennium: Form, Concept, and Theological Perspective*, ed. Wonil Kim et al., Studies in Antiquity & Christianity 2. Exegetical and Theological Studies (Harrisburg, PA: Trinity Press International, 2000), 273; Michael V. Fox, *Character and Ideology in the Book of Esther*, 2nd ed. (Columbia: University of South Carolina Press, 2001), 185.

38   Timothy K. Beal, *Esther, Berit Olam: Studies in Hebrew Narrative & Poetry*, ed. David W. Cotter (Collegeville, MN: Liturgical Press, 1999), 29. For a discussion of how prophetic literature sees a clear connection between Israelite worship of other gods and the loss of the presence of their true God, see Jill Middlemas, 'Divine Presence in Absence: Aniconism and Multiple Imaging in the Prophets', in *Divine Presence and Absence in Exilic and Post-Exilic Judaism: Studies of the Sofja Kovalevskaja Research Group on Early Monotheism* Vol 2, ed. Nathan MacDonald and Izaak J. de Hulster, FAT 61 (Tübingen: Mohr Siebeck, 2013), 185, 189.

39   Identical unvocalised niphal imperfect forms also occur in Gen 4:14; Job 13:20, and Ps 55:13.

phrase in the OT. The face of God (פְּנֵי אֱלֹהִים) or face of the Lord (פְּנֵי יהוה) are synonyms for divine presence (e.g. Exod 33:14). When God's faithful people 'seek his face' it is a desire to live in his presence (1 Chron 16:11), and this explains why it is a blessing to have 'the LORD make his face shine upon you' (Num 6:25). These connotations of intimacy are annulled when God hides his face, an act frequently associated with feelings of dismay and divine abandonment (e.g. Ps 10:11; 27:9; 30:7; 44:24 etc.). Thus, if there is a valid connection between Deut 31:18 and Esther on the matter of God's face being hidden, it is not evidence of benign and gracious divine providence operating in an understated way in the background. Rather, it connotes God's withdrawal from his unfaithful people.[40]

One advantage of explaining God's absence from the text as his judgement on the Jewish characters in the book is that it takes the absence of God seriously. Further, it sees divine absence producing theological opportunity rather than liability. Theologically speaking, the covenantal failings of God's people in Esther are the very sort of thing one might expect if the prophetic condemnation of Judah was justified. Rather than following the well-trodden path of insisting that the book affirms God's presence with his faithful people,[41] though in a hidden manner that requires generous interpretation of potential allusions to his presence or their faithfulness, one should acknowledge that this pietistic interpretation goes against the grain of the narrative. For in Esther, the characters

> do not seem to be looking for God at all! These are not good,
> pious people who cry out to God but feel they are being ignored,
> like the long-suffering Job. Mordecai and Esther are flawed Jews
> who deliver themselves and their people not by cleverness or

---

40 Tomasino finds more points of contact between Esther and Deut 31-32, thus potentially strengthening this point of view. Whether they establish any more firmly the larger point being argued–God's absence from Esther is his judgement on the Jews–is debatable. The points of contact and verbal similarities are not so acute as to demand a connection to Esther in particular. Further examples tend to be even more conjectural and concern incidental details rather than significant elements. See Anthony Tomasino, *Esther*, Evangelical Exegetical Commentary (Bellingham, WA: Lexham Press, 2016), 123-24.

41 For example, that 'one sees how [Esther and Mordecai's] faithfulness derives from their identity as persons in covenant with God, whose saving deeds on behalf of the Jews and the world make their lives possible', Newman, 'Where in the World Is God?', 180.

piety, but by taking advantage of the opportunities presented to them.[42]

There is no explicit evidence that they ever acknowledge God. Even in this supreme existential crisis of the potential obliteration of the Jews from the Persian empire, no Jewish prayers ascend to God. In Esther, the problem expressed by Jewish characters is not the absence of God but the presence of Haman. This does not mean that they are presented as rejecting God's existence, as if they were philosophical atheists, which would be historically anachronistic, but they appear to live as if God does not exist.[43] There were such people in the community of Israel. 'Fools say in their hearts, "There is no God" (Pss 14:1; 53:1; cf. Ps 10:4; Zeph 1:12).

Conclusion

We have investigated two approaches for reassessing Esther's potential contribution to biblical theology. The first was that Esther could make biblical-theological sense if one treated its unique 'godless' form not as an outright anomaly but as part of the clear, though neglected, OT theme of the increasingly reticent God. This would be a *theological* shift of perspective. Likewise, the second possibility would place the book within the mainstream of OT theology by re-evaluating its Jewish characters as being non-observant rather than exemplary. In

---

42 *Tomasino*, Esther, 121.
43 Within the Adventist tradition, Ellen White's infrequent references to the book generally make a more positive assessment of the Jews (e.g. 'The Return of the Exiles-No. 11: In the Days of Queen Esther', *Review and Herald*, 23 January 1908; *Prophets and Kings* (Mountain View, CA: Pacific Press, 1917). However, she never addresses the literary absence of God from the book, even though this was commonplace for nineteenth-century authors when writing for a comparable general readership (e.g. George Lawson, *Practical Expositions of the Whole Books of Ruth and Esther: With Three Sermons on the Duties of Parents to Their Children* [Philadelphia: W. S. Rentoul, 1870]; W. Burrows, *A Homiletical Commentary on the Book of Esther* [London: R. D. Dickinson, 1889]). If she had included this matter, it might well have nuanced her observations. Also, the interpretation suggested here is in line with how elsewhere in her writings she views God's role in judging Israel.

this, God's absence could be seen as a hiding of his face motivated by his people's unfaithfulness. This requires an *exegetical* shift in perspective.

These two approaches are presented here merely as examples of what might be done to rehabilitate Esther in the biblical-theological enterprise. Even if neither is deemed to be a perfect fit, I would suggest that one traditional approach is no longer fit for purpose. That is, the assertion that God is not absent from, and indeed can easily be found within, this book. Such conclusions usually derive from readers' initial aversions to Esther's 'godless' form, followed by understandable attempts to maintain the book as Scripture. However well intentioned, such endeavours underline an inability to understand a text that consistently and comprehensively fails to conform to biblical theistic norms. Yet it is these very aberrations that are fundamental to the book. Theological approaches to Esther which major on hunting down similarities between Esther and the rest of the canon, and treat the glaring difference—God's absence—as simply a detail of Esther's presentation utilised to underline God's hidden involvement in the background, do not, in my opinion, treat the text with enough respect. Too frequently, the similarities displayed by other biblical narratives, e.g. the Joseph story (a faithful Hebrew in a foreign court), or Exodus (the existence of God's people threatened but overcome), predetermine the interpretation of Esther. But this does not allow Esther to have a genuine dialogue with the rest of the canon, nor for its unique contribution to influence a comprehensive biblical theology. For the issue in Esther is not simply that God is absent and thus not explicitly involved with his people, but also that they never mention, worship, or attempt to interact with him. This is the book's unique contribution to the canon. What theological motivation could this narrator have possessed to compose a narrative that indirectly recalled biblical tradition, yet at the same time to eliminate any overt mention of Israel's faith? The absence not only of God, but also of any human spirituality, shows that the book's 'theology' , if that is an appropriate term, is more than just another permutation of conventional beliefs found throughout the OT. In this book, neither the Jews generally, nor Esther nor Mordecai individually, by anything they say or do, show any understanding of Israel's theological tradition. This reality needs to be incorporated into any biblical theology worthy of the name.

To Eat or Not To Eat
Food and Hubris in Daniel 1

Ivan Milanov

The rationale behind the decision of Daniel (and his three compatriots) not to defile themselves with the portion of food (*path-bag*)[1] and wine provided by King Nebuchadnezzar in Daniel 1:8 continues to attract the attention of the scholarly community. Some of the recently published articles on this topic, such as that of Michael Seufert,[2] confirm this observation. Seufert attempts to uncover the reason behind such a decision by exploring the intertextual links between Daniel 1 and Exodus 15-16. Despite proposing a novel intertextual analysis by linking Daniel 1 and Exodus 15-16, however, Seufert's article only treats a small portion of this topic.

I argue in this article that Daniel's refusal of the food and drink appointed by King Nebuchadnezzar is part of a much broader matrix of interrelated topics such as God's sovereignty, human hubris, divine–human conflict and the role of food in treating these topics in Daniel 1. By applying a combination of narrative criticism and intertextual analysis of Daniel 1 against the complex role of food decisions, both divine and human, in Genesis 1-2, I conclude that Daniel's refusal to eat the food assigned by the king is a refusal to accept Nebuchadnezzar's hubristic behaviour as the one who decides what humans should eat. I expect that this research will highlight a few theologically important points for

---

1   Path-bag is a Persian loanword, and it is best translated as 'portion of food'.
2   Michael Seufert, 'Refusing the King's Portion: A Reexamination of Daniel's Dietary Reaction in Daniel 1', *Journal for the Study of the Old Testament* (2019), vol. 43 (4), 644-60.

a more comprehensive understanding of the main themes in Daniel: the sovereignty of God and human acceptance of it.

The development of the argument will start with a critical evaluation of the existing interpretations regarding the possible reasons for Daniel's refusal of the daily portion of food and wine from King Nebuchadnezzar. There have been at least five different but sometimes related interpretations.

Scholarly Interpretations of Daniel's Refusal of the Food and Drink Appointed by the King

The most common explanation for the rationale for Daniel's refusal to consume the food and drink appointed by Nebuchadnezzar is that they contained meat of unclean animals or were not prepared in accordance with the instructions on how to prepare meat for consumption (Leviticus 11; Deuteronomy 14).[3] It seems that such an interpretation is incomplete. First, Daniel did not require meat of clean animals but rather he required 'vegetables to eat and water to drink' (Dan 1:12).[4] Second, the vegan food and water he requested from the chief of eunuchs came from Babylonian sources.[5] Third, Daniel refused to eat the meal even before he had had a chance to look at it and evaluate its content. Fourth, wine was not forbidden under the clean/unclean legislation in Torah. So, why, then, Daniel refused the wine remains unanswered by this interpretation.

Another scholarly explanation is that Daniel refused to consume the meal, because its content was firstly offered to the Babylonian deities as part of pagan worship.[6] However, this interpretation does not seem supported by the narrative in Daniel 1. First, food offering as part of pagan worship is not mentioned in the narrative at all. Second, vegetables or vegetable products were also attested as food used in worship services,[7] so why did Daniel reject the *path-bag* but requested vegetables?

---

[3] John J. Collins, *Daniel* (Minneapolis, MN: Augsburg, 1993), 142.
[4] Every quotation from the Hebrew Bible is my translation from the Masoretic Text published as *Biblia Hebraica Stuttgartensia* (Stuttgart: Deutsche Bibelgesellschaft, 1990).
[5] Carol Newsom, *Daniel* (Louisville, KY: Westminster John Knox, 2014), 48.
[6] André Lacocque, *The Book of Daniel* (Eugene, OR: Cascade, 2018), 48.
[7] Lev 2:1.

The ascetic reasons, similar to those of the Essenes and Hasidim, behind Daniel's refusal to defile himself with the food are the third possible interpretation.[8] Such ascetic preparation was important before one received God's revelation, as emphasised by the proponents of this interpretation. The main criticism of this explanation is that nowhere in Chapter 1 did Daniel and his friends receive any revelation in terms of vision and/or dreams (the first revelation takes place in Chapter 2). Further, Daniel used meat and wine as his usual diet later in the book (see 10:3). This excludes the idea that Daniel was a follower of ascetic ideology or its practitioner. Finally, Daniel had visions in Daniel 7-9, but it is not mentioned that he had fasted before receiving these revelations. It follows that fasting or abstaining from certain types of food before having a vision was the usual practice for Daniel.

The suggestion that Daniel refused the food because he did not want to lose his political independence is another interpretation put forward by certain scholars.[9] They argue that eating the king's food would mean entering into a covenant-style relationship with the king. However, the expression 'Daniel resolved that he would not defile himself' with the food appointed by the king has strong religious, even ritualistic, connotations in the first place. The verb גָּאַל denotes a physical defilement by either shedding someone's blood, both physically and metaphorically such as by taking a bribe (Isa 59:3; 63:3; Lam 4:13-14), or through ritual defilement by bringing unclean food to the Lord's table (Mal 1: 7, 12). Finally, Daniel did accept high political position in the Babylonian administration (Dan 1:19-21) and he demonstrated a special regard, even sympathy, for the kingship of Nebuchadnezzar (Dan 2:37-38; 4:19). So, Daniel was politically very much in line with the king's politics.

Seufert's interpretation includes some of the aspects of the previously mentioned 'political independence' interpretation but adds the arguments of the intertextual interpretation of Daniel 1 in relation to Exodus 15-16. The conclusion is that Daniel's refusal of the food and wine appointed by Nebuchadnezzar is 'a clear counter-claim to the king's assertions of absolute authority over' Daniel and his three compatriots.[10] He concludes that such research 'points to the multi-layered significance of Daniel's abstention from the king's portion, namely,

---

8   Lacocque, *Daniel*, 50.
9   Ernest C. Lucas, *Daniel* (Leicester: Inter-Varsity Press, 2002), 54.
10   Seufert, 'Refusing the King's Portion', 644.

both a ritual concern attending the exiles and a statement from Daniel that Yahweh is his only provider, contrary to Nebuchadnezzar's claim'.[11] Although I generally agree with Seufert's conclusion, my main criticism would be that more attention should be paid to the narrative features in Daniel 1. For instance, the food and drink which Daniel requested and accepted came from King Nebuchadnezzar (not from the sky, as did the manna), but that type of food and drink was not appointed by the king. In other words, the king was again the provider, but his order was disobeyed. This was clearly pointed out by the chief of eunuchs (v.10). So, the issue is not who the provider was (there is no doubt that King Nebuchadnezzar was) but who had the authority to appoint or decide what kind of food and drink should be consumed by Daniel and his compatriots.

The above evaluation demonstrates that none of the interpretations mentioned are comprehensive enough in terms of offering plausible exegetical and theological solutions for the rationale behind Daniel's decision not to defile himself with the food and drink appointed by King Nebuchadnezzar. The common characteristic of all above-mentioned interpretations is that the focus of the argumentation is mainly on the intertextual links outside of the book of Daniel, but the dynamics of the relationships between God, King Nebuchadnezzar, Daniel and his compatriots in the narrative of Daniel 1 seem neglected in the interpretation process. Therefore, I aim to present a comprehensive explanation of the rationale behind Daniel's decision not to defile himself with the appointed food that stems from the narrative in Daniel 1 and its intertextual links with Genesis 1-2; Leviticus 11; and Deuteronomy 14. The rivalry pairs in Daniel 1 serve as the starting point for my interpretation.

---

11   Seufert, 'Refusing the King's Portion', 644.

The Rivalry Between God and Nebuchadnezzar in Daniel 1:1-2

Nebuchadnezzar	Jehoiakim
Babylon	Jerusalem
Land of Shinar	Judah
The Treasure House of Nebuchadnezzar's god	Jerusalem's Temple
Nebuchadnezzar's god	Lord

Table 1

The above paradigm demonstrates how a political/military conflict is related to the realm of religion. The conflict between Nebuchadnezzar and Jehoiakim is intrinsically associated with a religious conflict/contest. Consequently, the religious conflict/contest in Daniel 1.1-2 points to a divine conflict: The Babylonian (Nebuchadnezzar's) god vs. the Lord (יְיָאֲ). The characterisation of both deities, Babylonian and Judean, announces a very specific contest between them. Overall, in comparison to God's characterisation, the Babylonian god's characterisation is extremely poor and, in some sense, reflects the narrator's attitude towards the Babylonian deity.

For instance, the narrator neither informs the reader regarding the name of the Babylonian god, nor attributes to him any act, emotion, speech or other device of characterisation. An omission of a character's name in the narratives, according to Adele Berlin, is the lowest level of characterisation.[12] Without a name or any other attribute or act ascribed to the Babylonian deity, it seems that he exists as a character merely depending on Nebuchadnezzar's point of view. The narrator does not portray the king's deity as an independent character in the narrative who exists in his own right.

Depriving the Babylonian god of a name and of ascribing any act or speech to him, the narrator makes this deity passive and uninvolved in the events described in the narrative. This reduced characterisation of Nebuchadnezzar's deity may reveal the narrator's suspicion of his existence or, at least, the narrator portrays the Babylonian deity as a character who is ignorant towards the events in the narrative.

---

12   Adele Berlin, *Poetics and Interpretation of Biblical Narrative* (Winona Lake, IN: Eisenbrauns, 1994), 99-101.

On the other hand, the narrator presents the Lord (אֲדֹנָי) as a character whose acts have a crucial influence on the most dramatic points of the story. The Lord gives (נָתַן) Nebuchadnezzar the victory over his Judean counterpart Jehoiakim. The two references 'God gave' (נָתַן) in Daniel 1:9, 17 indicate very important events in the life of Daniel and his three compatriots. All these acts of God are of immense importance in the narrative, and they significantly shape the dynamics of the conflict, because the God of Israel is always portrayed as the one who controls the events and gives Daniel and his compatriots success in everything despite their being exiles from Judah.

It could be concluded that at the very beginning the narrator gives a minimum of characterisation to Nebuchadnezzar's god. In particular, the king's god is presented as a passive and ignorant deity as opposed to the omnipotent and active God of the Jews. This creates conditions for the existence of a new rivalry, where the king remains the only rival to God.

The Rivalry Between God and Nebuchadnezzar in Daniel 1:3-21

Danna N. Fewell[13] is right when she states that the paradigm of rivalry pairs is changed in this portion of the narrative:

Nebuchadnezzar	God
Nebuchadnezzar's servants	God's servants

Table 2

Jehoiakim and the geographic locations (cities: Jerusalem and Babylon, and lands: Judah and Shinar), along with Nebuchadnezzar's deity, are no longer part of the narrative in Daniel 1:3-21. Nebuchadnezzar's deity neither participates in the following events, nor is a specific role or act ascribed to Nebuchadnezzar's deity in the narrative beyond Daniel 1:1-2. The ultimate authority, therefore, who remains on the side opposite to God is the king of Babylon. The new rivalry between Nebuchadnezzar and God, which begins in Daniel 1:3 and develops onwards, creates preconditions for committing hubris.

The rivalry between Nebuchadnezzar and God in 1.3 onwards is overtly of a religious nature. This brief analysis of the nature of the conflict/contest in

---

13   Danna N. Fewell, *Circle of Sovereignty: Plotting Politics in the Book of Daniel* (Nashville, TN: Abingdon, 1991), 21.

Daniel 1:1-21 implies several points of importance for the study of the concept of hubris in Daniel 1. First, the gods of Babylon, though mentioned in Daniel 1:2, are inactive in any of the events of Daniel 1. The narrator does not ascribe a single act to them. Since the Babylonian gods are inactive and are not portrayed, unlike the God of the Judeans, the only remaining rival to God in Daniel 1 is Nebuchadnezzar. The conflict/contest in Daniel 1, therefore, is actually between God and Nebuchadnezzar, between the divine and the human.

Second, from the very beginning the narrator emphasises that God is in absolute control over the world of the narrative in Daniel 1. He is responsible for Nebuchadnezzar's victory over Jehoiakim, and God later successfully thwarts Nebuchadnezzar's order regarding the appointment of the food.[14] This leads us to the conclusion that Nebuchadnezzar's royal sovereignty is of a delegated nature. He is not an authority in himself, but he is being given authority from God. Nebuchadnezzar's orders are not as important as God's and God is able to change the king's plans.

What Did Daniel Require as an Alternative to the Food and Drink Appointed by King Nebuchadnezzar?

This is one of the key issues in determining the reason behind Daniel's refusal of the appointed food. The key terms are 'vegetables' and 'to appoint'. Daniel refused to be defiled by the food and wine appointed by Nebuchadnezzar due to his resolve to reject Nebuchadnezzar as a divine authority. First, in 1:12 Daniel requested food (מִזְרֹעִים in plural; it is *hapax legomenon* usually translated as 'vegetables') that resembles God's appointed food in Gen 1:29: 'all herbs yielding seed' (עֵשֶׂב זֹרֵעַ זֶרַע). The noun מִזְרֹעִים (זֵרֹעַ in the singular) of Daniel 1:12

---

[14] Daniel and his compatriots have been approved a diet according to their request by the court officials without permission from Nebuchadnezzar. God has the key role in this event as he 'gave Daniel to find kindness and mercy before the chief eunuch' (Daniel 1:9) God reacts to the choice of Daniel, Azariah, Mishael and Hananiah by giving them wisdom and knowledge that impress Nebuchadnezzar. It seems that the young Jews succeed by ignoring the king's order (Daniel 1:10-20).

has the same consonants as עֶרֶן (seed) in Genesis 1:29. So, Daniel requested the type of food that God, the creator, had given to the first humans.

Second, God as the ultimate creator has the exclusive right to appoint the food for humans (Gen 1:29; 2:16-17; 9:3-4; Lev 11; Deut 14). Ignoring such appointment had certain consequences (Gen 2:17). On the other hand, practising God's commandment regarding diet was a demonstration of the Israelites' special relationship with God (Lev 11: 44-45; Deut 14:21). Third, the verb denoting Nebuchadnezzar's act of appointing food is מָנָה in *Piel*. This verb could denote a royal authority in appointing officials (1 Chron 9:29) in the *Pu'al* participle.

However, the verb הִנָּה in Piel is attested in Jonah 2:1; 4:6-8 as a description of God's authority and power over created beings (e.g. fish, worms) and plants. A similar usage occurs in Aramaic in Daniel 5:25-26 as a description of God's power to appoint kings. Thus, the narrator describes Nebuchadnezzar's act as an attempt to usurp the authority and power of God.

Theological Implications of Nebuchadnezzar's Hubris in Daniel 1

There are at least three plausible implications that could be drawn from Nebuchadnezzar's hubris and the way in which God responds to it. First, the act of hubris contributes to the presentation of the concept of monotheism in the book of Daniel with at least two features: (1) the attempt at hubris is always directed towards the God of Israel, and (2) the attempts at hubris are exclusively carried out by humans. The first feature excludes any other deity in the rank of the God of Israel. The second one presents humans as the highest authorities that attempt acts of hubris; the exclusive rival of God in Daniel 1 is a human ruler. Along with hints at the inactivity and non-existence of pagan gods, these two features significantly contribute to the narrator's presentation that there is only one God–the God of Israel.

Further, the presentation of the hubris of Nebuchadnezzar in Daniel 1 contains strong anti-idolatry implications. In its essence, the attempt of hubris represents the act of substituting God with a human being and their religious/ethical standards, and/or their achievements. The actual anti-idolatry statement is seen in Daniel's refusal to defile himself with the appointed food. The relationship between the cause (the royal hubris) and effect (the reaction of Daniel) has a precise structure and a clear anti-idolatry message.

Finally, the hubristic behaviour of Nebuchadnezzar in appointing food and drink for Daniel and his compatriots (Dan 1:5) is met by refusal (v. 8) and eventual disobedience of the king's command (v. 16). This demonstrates that Nebuchadnezzar is not able to challenge God's sovereignty seriously. The king is human and as such he is no match for God's superiority. On the contrary, the conflict between the king and God in Daniel 1 results in God's powerful demonstrations of himself as the ultimate authority and power: the king's command is derailed, but God makes Daniel and his compatriots prosper.

Conclusion

In the light of the previous analysis it could be concluded that Daniel and his compatriots are more concerned with the authority who has appointed the food than with the type of food. That Nebuchadnezzar remains the only rival to God in the conflict/contest in Daniel 1 implies that the king's act of appointing the food and drink is understood by the narrator and Daniel as denoting a person who claims a creational authority similar to that of God. It seems that Nebuchadnezzar is described in Daniel 1:5 as the one who gives orders from a position of divine authority (see Gen 1:29; 2:16-17). In other words, Nebuchadnezzar's act of appointing the food and drink represents the narrator's description, shared by Daniel and his compatriots, that the king is attempting to act in a fashion reserved, at least from the point of view of the narrator and the Jewish characters, for the God of Israel. And, by definition, this is hubristic behaviour. Such a depiction of royal hubris has strong monotheistic and anti-idolatry implications.

Living in the Post-Easter Era
The Theology of the Matthean Eschatological Discourse (Matthew 24-25)

Laszlo Gallusz

Despite the masterful character and strong influence of the First Gospel both in Jewish- and Gentile-Christian communities of the early church, its author, Matthew, is not considered by contemporary authors to be one of the pre-eminent theologians of the first century, in rank with Paul and John. While his literary creativity is beyond discussion,[1] it has been argued that his theological thinking is not hallmarked by innovation, as is that of the above mentioned two apostles.[2] Nevertheless, the Matthean version of the Eschatological Discourse (chs. 24-25) provides the theologically richest glimpse in Jesus' teaching on the eschaton in the New Testament.[3] This notorious and much debated text is full of interpretative difficulties. A lot of ink has been spilt over issues such as the cryptic 'abomination of desolation' (βδέλυγμα τῆς ἐρημώσεως; 24:15),[4] the relationship of the destruction of the temple and the parousia, the great tribulation,

---

1   See e.g. Jack Dean Kingsbury, *Matthew as Story* (Philadelphia, PA: Fortress, 1986); John Nolland, *The Gospel of Matthew: A Commentary on the Greek Text*, NIGTC (Grand Rapids, MI: Eerdmans; Carlisle: Paternoster, 2005), 23-29.
2   W. D. Davies and Dale C. Allison, *A Critical Commentary on the Gospel According to Saint Matthew*, ICC, 3 vols. (London: T&T Clark, 1997), 3:722; R. Alan Culpepper, *Matthew*, NTL (Louisville, KY: Westminster John Knox, 2021), 19.
3   The Markan and Lukan versions are significantly shorter: they are respectively 37 and 32 verses long, as compared with the 97 verses of Matthew.
4   All the biblical texts in this chapter are taken from NRSV, unless otherwise stated, as in this case.

the problem of 'this generation' (24:34) etc.[5] In some Christian circles, the discourse has served and still serves as the foundational text for cataloguing the 'signs of the times' which are seen as heralding the impending parousia.

While a number of detailed studies have been published in the last several decades on Matthew 24-25, the theological exploration of the discourse has been largely neglected.[6] One of the rare exceptions is the work of Barna, who examines the discourse by employing a theological-thematic reading which he sees as a 'complementary' and 'necessary' step to the exegetical work.[7] His study is, however, focused on the discussion of the problem of signs of the parousia in ch. 24, hence no attention is given to the theological investigation of the discourse as a whole. Talbert also explores, in his commentary, theological matters related to the Matthean Eschatological Discourse, but his approach is selective: he concentrates mainly on the apocalyptic pattern of Matthew's eschatology.[8] Similar selectivity is characteristic of the work of Luz, whose theological enquiry focuses on Matthew's judgement theology.[9] Furthermore, a number of comprehensive earlier studies, such as those by Ladd, Ridderbos or Berkouwer, discuss

---

5   The Matthean version of the Eschatological Discourse has received incomparably less scholarly attention than the Markan version, because of the influence of source critical discussions.

6   Some of the major studies are the following: Fred W. Burnett, *The Testament of Jesus-Sophia: A Redactional-Critical Study of the Eschatological Discourse in Matthew* (Washington, DC: University Press of America, 1981); Victor K. Agbanou, *Le Discours Eschatologique de Matthieu 24-25: Tradition et Rédaction* (Paris: Libraire Lecoffre, 1983); David Wenham, *Gospel Perspectives: The Rediscovery of Jesus' Eschatological Discourse*. Volume IV (Sheffield: JSOT Press, 1984); Jeffrey A. Gibbs, *Jerusalem and Parousia: Jesus' Eschatological Discourse in Matthew's Gospel* (Saint Louis, MI: Concordia Academic Press, 2000); Alistair I. Wilson, *When Will These Things Happen? A Study of Jesus as Judge in Matthew 21-25*, Paternoster Biblical Monographs (Eugene, OR: Wipf and Stock, 2006).

7   Jan Barna, 'The Progression in the Signs of the Parousia in the Eschatological Speeches of Jesus' , in *Eschatology from an Adventist Perspective: Proceedings of the Fourth International Bible Conference*. Rome, 11-20 June, 2018, eds. Elias Brasil de Souza et al. (Silver Springs, MD: Biblical Research Institute, 2021), 139-60.

8   Charles H. Talbert, *Matthew*, Paideia (Grand Rapids, MI: Baker Academic, 2010), 278-81.

9   Ulrich Luz, *The Theology of the Gospel of Matthew*, New Testament Theology, trans. J. Bradford Robinson (Cambridge: Cambridge University Press, 1995), 125-32.

theologically the Eschatological Discourse, but without nuancing carefully the contribution of each of the three synoptic authors.[10]

This study seeks to break fresh ground in the theological reading of the discourse by paying attention to Matthew 24-25 as a literary and theological whole. It aims to identify and investigate the cardinal theological themes of the discourse giving insight into the rhetorical agenda of Matthew. It argues that Jesus' use of apocalyptic language in the discourse is not given for speculation over the future, but rather for ethical-ecclesial purposes: to help the disciples to live attentively and responsibly in the presence of the one who has come and who will come.

Before we turn to the discussion of the theological themes of the Matthean Eschatological Discourse, necessary preparatory work needs to be done. First, the wider theological context of the discourse will be briefly explored, since the Eschatological Discourse is not to be approached as an isolated text. Second, the arrangement of the discourse will be examined. Both of these steps have important implications for the task of the theological interpretation of Matthew 24-25, which will be undertaken as the third step in the course of this investigation.

Jesus' Kingdom Theology and the Eschatological Discourse

According to Matthew, the theological centre point of Jesus' teaching (διδάσκειν) and proclamation (κηρύσσειν) was 'the good news of the kingdom' (τὸ εὐαγγέλιον τῆς βασιλείας; 4:23; 9:35).[11] The proclamation of 'this good news of the kingdom' is mentioned also in the Eschatological Discourse (24:14) referring to the mission of the church in the post-Easter era.[12] As announced by Jesus, this theme implies the arrival of God's eschatological kingship with its two distinct aspects: the kingdom as a present reality established in this world (immanent dynamic dominion of God) and its future manifestation (transcendent spatial

---

10 George Eldon Ladd, *The Presence of the Future: The Eschatology of Biblical Realism* (Grand Rapids, MI: Eerdmans, 1974), 3-42; Herman Ridderbos, T*he Coming of the Kingdom*, trans. H. de Jongste (Philadelphia, PA: Presbyterian and Reformed, 1975), 477-97; G. C. Berkouwer, *The Return of Christ*, Studies in Dogmatics (Grand Rapids, MI: Eerdmans, 1972), 235-59.
11 The same expression (τοῦτο τὸ εὐαγγέλιον τῆς βασιλείας) is found also in 26:13.
12 Matthew 26:13 has the shorter version of 'this good news'.

kingdom).[13] Both aspects of the kingdom have strong eschatological overtones, and they are integral stages in the fulfilment of God's plan. The human existence between the Christ-event and the parousia takes place in the tension of the 'now-but-not-yet' in which God's promises are realised, but not fully extended.

In this connection, the Eschatological Discourse is highly significant, because it provides an extended discussion on the coming of the future reign of God. This coming has already been referred to in Matthew's gospel in a number of ways: (1) in the 'Your kingdom come' petition of the Lord's Prayer (6:10); (2) in statements about 'entry' into the kingdom (5:20; 7:21; 18:3) and its opposite of 'being cast out' (7:2; 8:12; 13:42, 50; 22:13; cf. 24:51; 25:11, 30); (3) in expressions on inheriting (eternal) life (19:29); (4) in the image of the promised land (5:5); (5) in references to the future judgment (5:3, 10; cf. 25:34); (6) in the expression 'for the sake of the kingdom of heaven' (19:12; cf. 19:29); (7) in using future tenses with 'in the kingdom' (5:19; 13:43); (8) in the statement on the coming of the Son of Man in his glory (16:27); and (9) in major images such as the great banquet prepared by God (8:11; 22:11-13; cf. 25:1-12, 21, 23), the harvest (13:24-30), and the pictures of the catch of fish (13:47) or the leavened mass (13:33).[14] Clearly, in these images and expressions a culmination in the fulfilment of the coming of God's perfect kingdom is envisioned and an appeal is made which stresses the value of living in the perspective of the eschatological hope.

Since Matthew portrays Jesus primarily as a teaching Messiah, the 'messianic teacher of wisdom',[15] it is natural to expect that his discourses address not only the kingdom life which had already arrived in his earthly ministry, but also the divine purpose that leads to the full realisation of the kingdom. The Eschatological Discourse, which is the second longest discourse of the five discourses in the First Gospel, provides this final capstone in Jesus' multifaceted

---

13 The understanding of the coming of the kingdom was an intensive debate in 20th-century scholarship. For an overview of the history of research, see Ladd, *Presence*, 3-42.

14 For a somewhat different categorisation, see Rudolf Schnackenburg, *God's Rule and Kingdom*, 2nd ed. (New York: Herder and Herder; London: Burns and Oates, 1968), 160-63.

15 Martin Hengel, *Studies in Early Christology* (Edinburgh: T&T Clark, 1995), 73-117. For the tradition of the teaching Messiah in ancient Judaism, see e.g. Isa 11:2-4; 1 En 49:1-3; 51:3; Pss. Sol. 17:43; 4Q521 frag. 2.1-2; Tg. Isa. 42:1; 53:5, 11-12.

kingdom theology.[16] As such, its detailed discussion is of utmost importance for understanding the great divine work of salvation and the human response to it embodied in the idea of entering into or failing to enter the kingdom of heaven.

The Arrangement of the Eschatological Discourse

The complexity of structuring the Matthean Eschatological Discourse is noteworthy. It is almost impossible to find two authors who agree on all the details.[17] The basic problem is that Matthew seems to move freely between describing the impending crisis (the destruction of Jerusalem) and the end of the age (the parousia). Mounce calls our attention to the fact that 'it is not uncommon for prophetic material to move between type and antitype without calling attention to exactly what is happening.'[18] So, the fluidity of the discourse reflects the author's own setting, rather than sharing our contemporary western concern for meticulous, orderly continuity.

Still, I suggest, there are clear structural indicators in the text which signal the flow of the argument and consequently the main sections of the discourse. First, the discourse starts with a narrative introductory scene which provides the setting for what follows: Jesus' prediction about the destruction of temple and the double question of the disciples (24:1-3).[19] Second, in a didactic section, Jesus focuses on human history by delineating events on earth and in heaven

---

16 Surprisingly, the Eschatological Discourse is almost completely ignored by some scholars in reconstructing the theology of Matthew. See e.g. Peter Stuhlmacher, *Biblical Theology of the New Testament*, trans. Daniel P. Bailey (Grand Rapids, MI: Eerdmans, 2018). Similarly, Barry D. Smith (*Jesus' Twofold Teaching About the Kingdom of God*, NTM 24 [Sheffield: Sheffield Phoenix, 2009]) overlooks the Eschatological Discourse in discussing Jesus' kingdom theology. The reason for this ignorance might lie in the fact that Jesus' primary emphasis was on the present aspect of the kingdom and not so much on its future coming.

17 I came to this conclusion by examining about thirty major commentaries, monographs and scholarly articles which discuss the structure of the discourse.

18 Robert H. Mounce, *Matthew*, NIBC (Peabody, MA: Hendrickson; Carlisle: Paternoster, 1991), 222.

19 Matthew 23 provides a wider setting, though there is a shift from a wider audience (the crowd and his disciples; 23:1) to a private one (his disciples only; 24:1, 3). Burnett (*Testament*, 21-25) considers that the discourse begins at 24:4, but the narrative introduction of 24:1-2 is related contextually to the Eschatological Discourse and also to the discourse of Woes in ch. 23 which provides a bridge between the two.

followed by the parousia (24:4-31). Third, in a paraenetic section, Jesus exhorts the disciples by stressing the importance of vigilance (24:32-25:30). Fourth, in a scene of the final judgement, human accountability is emphasised and the theme of living appropriately in the light of the coming eschaton is continued (25:31-46). On the basis of this macro-structure, it seems that 24:32 constitutes the 'hinge' of the Eschatological Discourse, because it draws a line between the didactic and paraenetic sections.[20] In the first, the emphasis is on the expected events, while in the second the church is urged to respond in vigilance and preparation for the coming eschaton. The paraenetic section is longer: 50 verses (and an additional 16 verses of the final judgement scene), as compared to the 28 verses of the didactic section. This difference in length is not insignificant for uncovering the rhetorical purpose of the author.

This analysis demonstrates that any comprehensive theological analysis of Matthew 24-25 which focuses on the events preceding the eschaton, the eschaton itself, the judgement or simply on discipleship, is incomplete and one-sided. The structure indicates that while the discourse has an eschatological overtone, end-expectation and the conception of church are strictly indivisible. Thus eschatology and ecclesiology are closely related in the discourse, which is not surprising, because no other Gospel is as strongly shaped by the concept of church as is the First Gospel.[21] Since discipleship is to be understood not only as an ecclesiological concept, but also as an experiential reality linked to the person

---

[20] Though Gibb's (*Jerusalem*, 174-176) interpretation of the Parousia in terms of first-century events is problematic, he correctly maintains that 24:36 is the dividing line between the two cardinal sections of the discourse.

[21] Günther Bornkamm, Gerhard Barth and Heinz Joachim Held (*Tradition and Interpretation in Matthew* [London: SCM, 1963], 15-24) rightly note that all discourses in the Gospel of Matthew have an eschatological slant in which end-expectation and the concept of church are closely linked.

of Jesus, Christology must also be given some consideration in the theological analysis of Matthew 24-25.

Theological Themes

In the following, I will discuss five cardinal theological themes featuring in Matthew 24-25. I will aim to uncover how they are woven into the material of the discourse and how they are linked together.

The Fairness of God: Justice and Judgement

The Eschatological Discourse is impregnated with the theme of God's justice as expressed in judgement. In the Matthean worldview, both the righteous and the wicked are to face consequences for their deeds in this world.[22] On the one hand, seeking first the kingdom and its righteousness results in experiencing God's care (6:33); moreover, the righteous 'will inherit the earth' (5:5). On the other hand, like Sodom and Gomorrah which were destroyed because of their wickedness (11:23), Jerusalem must count on judgement (21:18-19; 22:7; 24:2) because of its history of rejecting messengers sent by God.[23] The deeds-consequences line of reasoning is strongly present in the Eschatological Discourse. Surprisingly, this is overlooked by Reiser, who fails to consider the discourse in constructing the judgement theology of Jesus as reflected in the Synoptic Gospels.[24]

The wider literary context of the Eschatological Discourse is of vital importance for understanding the judgement theology of Matthew 24-25. Indeed, 24:1-2 functions as the culmination of the theme of God's judgement upon

---

22 Anders Runesson (*Divine Wrath and Salvation in Matthew: The Narrative World of the First Gospel* [Minneapolis, MN: Fortress, 2016], 165-71) suggests that these deeds can be categorised as 'external deeds' (e.g. 'good fruit' or hospitality-3:10; 7:17-19; 10:40-42), 'verbal deeds' (e.g. insults, blasphemy or careless words-5:22; 12:32, 36) and 'internal deeds' (things that happen in secret–6:2-4, 16-18). On divine justice as equivalent to the repayment of deeds in Matthean thought, see Cedric E. W. Vine, *Jesus and the Nations: Discipleship and Mission in the Gospel of Matthew* (Eugene, OR: Pickwick, 2022), 141-43.
23 Vine (*Jesus*, 62) notes: 'The destruction of Jerusalem is thereby related to the history of the people of Israel and the justice of God.'
24 Marius Reiser, *Jesus and Judgment: The Eschatological Proclamation in its Jewish Context*, trans. Linda M. Maloney (Minneapolis, MN: Fortress, 1997).

Israel as foreshadowed in chs. 21-23.[25] As the narrative progresses, the emphasis on the judgement on Israel becomes increasingly stronger (21:23, 31, 43), until the judgement oracle of the Woes is uttered in ch. 23. Climactic to it is Jesus' abandoning of the temple (24:1) which is preceded by the statement: 'See, your house is left to you, desolate' (23:3). The account is reminiscent of Ezekiel's vision of the departing of God's glory from the temple (Ezek 10:18-19), particularly since a link is made with the Mount of Olives (Ezek 11:22-23; cf. Matt 24:3).[26] So, even if Matthew 23 is a separate discourse from chs. 24-25, it is intricately linked to it, thematically providing a theological clue to its interpretation.

Not only is the starting point of the Eschatological Discourse a judgement oracle (24:1-2), but so is its concluding scene (25:31-46). Namely, the Eschatological Discourse ends with a portrayal of the universal final judgement conducted by the Son of Man sitting 'on the throne of his glory' (25:31).[27] This scene reflects an apocalyptic awareness according to which justice will prevail at the end and no one will be able to escape it. This provides grounds for confidence in the future, an incentive to look forward to God's radical transformation of the present order of things, and to the coming of the eschatological kingdom that includes no trace of evil.[28]

In addition to the beginning and the end of the discourse, its heart, the parousia scene (24:29-31), also resonates with the notion of judgement. Davies and Allison appropriately name this scene 'the dramatic zenith' of the discourse.[29] The cosmic 'shaking' (σαλευθήσονται), described in the Day of the Lord language drawn from the Old Testament, implies that all quake, since the Son of Man comes as a judge and ruler over all things (cf. 16:27; 19:28; 25:31).[30] The

---

25 Burnett, *Testament*, 22-23.
26 Wilson, *When*, 135.
27 In opposition to this view, Chad Venters (*The Sheep and the Goats: A Matthean Teaching in Historical Context* [Lanham: Lexington and Fortress Academic, 2022], 4) argues that 25:31-46 does not describe 'the end of the space continuum-time continuum, rather it was to build on the theme of judgment against Israel when her temple fell'. This hypothesis is built on parallels with Psalm 80, but it fails to take seriously the eschatological language which permeates the discourse and the character of the Matthean theology of judgement developed throughout the book.
28 Margaret Davies, *Matthew*, Readings Series (Sheffield: JSOT Press, 1993), 175.
29 Davies and Allison, *Matthew*, 3:358.
30 For a detailed study on the background of Matthew's catastrophe language, see e.g. Edward Adams, *Stars Will Fall From Heaven: Cosmic Catastrophe in the New Testament and Its World*, LNTS 347 (London: T&T Clark, 2007).

parousia brings 'a mighty reversal of fortunes', reflecting the materialisation of God's justice (24:31).³¹

Thus, the Eschatological Discourse sees judgement as integral to God's plan. It is made clear that there are lesser judgements as well as the final judgement of God, and the two are related. As De Pressensé notes, 'Every period has its own decisive event, and receives its own solemn sentence. These partial judgements foretell the great and final judgement.'³² At the end, divine justice is inescapable, because it is the reflection of the moral structure of the universe rooted in God's fairness.

Time of Woes, Time of Hope: Interpretation of History

Matthew portrays a fundamentally apocalyptic picture of history. The present is seen as evil and dark: a time of woes likened to 'birth pangs' (ὠδῖνες; 24:8). Interpreting the current era and the immediate past in terms of the messianic woes is not unique to Matthew. Allison calls our attention to the fact that such an outlook can also be established in the Testament of Moses, portions of the Dead Sea Scrolls, 4 Ezra, Mark and Revelation.³³

The 'time of woes' appears to be an extended period which involves continuous suffering, but it is also marked by a worldwide proclamation of the 'good news of the kingdom' (24:14). In this age not only has love grown cold (24:12), but the people of God are to live with false prophets (24:11, 23-28), experiencing hate and tribulation (24:9). Additionally, they are to witness catastrophes including Israel's national catastrophe. From a phenomenon of 'abomination of desolation' (24:15), the fulfilment of a Danielic prediction, one can only try to flee.³⁴ Essentially, the Eschatological Discourse defines 'the character of time as

---

31 G. B. Caird, *Jesus and the Jewish Nation* (London: Athlone Press, 1965), 20.
32 Quoted in George R. Beasley-Murray, *Jesus and the Last Days: The Interpretation of the Olivet Discourse* (Vancouver: Regent, 1993), 129.
33 For details, see Dale C. Allison, *The End of the Ages has Come: An Early Interpretation of the Passion and Resurrection of Jesus* (Philadelphia, PA: Fortress, 1985), 7-14, 26-39, 70-73.
34 As Vine (*Jesus*, 47) notes, Jesus' command to 'flee to the mountains' echoes the command to Lot to 'flee to the hills' without looking back and stopping anywhere (Gen 19:17). For an in-depth discussion of the 'abomination of desolation', see Desmond Ford, *The Abomination of Desolation in*

one of "crisis".[35] As Luz notes, 'Matthew paints his own present black because he no longer sees a future for the world'–things have gone beyond the point of repair.[36]

An exclusively negative view of history in Matthew 24-25 must be tempered by an often overlooked aspect. Namely, the darkness of evil does not prevail in the narrative, but it is counterbalanced by the great hope for the parousia of the glorified Christ (24:29-44). While the immediate future is horrific, the ultimate future is glorious. I suggest that God's people are prompted by the Eschatological Discourse to relate to the future as to a time of woes and time of hope at the same time. Affliction is to be seen as only the prelude to God's vindication of his people and his transformation of the present evil world. The fact that human history is pictured as moving in the direction of the final solution of the problem of evil, despite the troublesome experiences of God's people, provides an assurance that would have encouraged Matthew's original audience to persevere in faithfulness and hope.[37] While they were prepared by the discourse for a dramatic time marked by a long haul, they were also ensured that living in a waiting mode is made possible because of a hope made real–a hope grounded not in illusion, but in the reality of Jesus' promise.[38]

So, the Eschatological Discourse defines the character of human history by reinforcing hope in the midst of overwhelming despair. The hardships are not indefinite and they will not last forever. While the present evil age inflicts

---

Biblical Eschatology (Washington, DC: University Press of America, 1979); Michael Theophilos, The Abomination of Desolation in Matthew 24.15, LNTS 437 (London: T & T Clark, 2012).

35 Ridderbos, *Coming*, 477.
36 Ulrich Luz, *Matthew: A Commentary*, Hermeneia, 3 vols. (Minneapolis, MN: Fortress, 1989-2005), 3:206.
37 Davies, Matthew, 175-176. Similarly, Michael Green (*The Message of Matthew: The Kingdom of Heaven, The Bible Speaks Today* [Downers Grove, IL: Inter-Varsity, 2000], 48) notes that according to the Eschatological Discourse 'the world is moving not towards chaos, though there will be plenty of that (24:3-31), but towards Christ and his return. Every moment worth its salt has an eschatology, an expectation of how it will all end.'
38 Stanley Hauerwas, *Matthew*, SCM Theological Commentary on the Bible (London: SCM, 2006), 207.

wounds on God's people, hope is nurtured 'by showing how a good future can issue from an evil present'.[39]

Christ and the Eschaton

The Eschatological Discourse presents Jesus not only as a teacher, but as a prophet who foresees the eschatological future. This Christological perspective is not new. Throughout the entire Gospel Jesus prophesies events related to the end-time scenario: the activity of false prophets (7:15-23), the persecution of disciples (10:21-39), the coming of the Son of Man (16:27) and the angelic harvest (13:49). The Eschatological Discourse clarifies these details and enlarges them significantly.

In the discourse itself, Jesus appears as a messianic-eschatological figure with a crucial role in history. While the rest of the Gospel emphasises the 'newness of the new situation created by Jesus' coming'[40] and his function in the era which he has inaugurated, in Matthew 24 he is portrayed as the Son of Man 'coming on the clouds of heaven with power and great glory' (24:30).[41] This coming, the parousia, represents the ultimate triumph of God's plan. This triumph is solidly grounded in the death and resurrection of Jesus, and it will be made complete by the termination of the order of evil when the Son of Man will publicly reveal his kingly rule over the universe. Although a throne is not specifically mentioned in 24:29-31, the fact that he is 'coming on the clouds of heaven' (ἐρχόμενον ἐπὶ τῶν νεφελῶν τοῦ οὐρανοῦ; 24:30) is telling: The Son of Man is pictured as coming 'with the clouds of heaven' (עִם־עֲנָנֵי שְׁמַיָּא) to the Ancient One in Daniel 7:13.[42] Not less significantly, during the exodus the Shekinah presence of God guided Israel in a cloud by day and in a fire at night (Exod 13:21-22; 14:24); later the Shekinah glory covered the sanctuary as a cloud (Exod 40:34-38). In the

---

39 Davies and Allison, *Matthew*, 3:328
40 Nolland, *Matthew*, 41.
41 The 'Son of Man' title is found only on the lips of Jesus. The meaning of the title was one of the most significant debates of the last century in New Testament scholarship. For a recent comprehensive overview of the discussion and the main interpretative possibilities, see e.g. Craig D. Saunders, A Mediator in *Matthew: An Analysis of the Son of Man's Function in the First Gospel* (Eugene, OR: Pickwick, 2021), 2-29.
42 Tremper Longman (*Daniel*, NIVAC [Grand Rapids, MI: Zondervan, 1999], 186-88) notes parallels with the 'divine cloud-rider' motif in the OT and outside of it–a language used consistently for the designation of a deity itself.

light of these Old Testament backgrounds, the Son of Man's parousia 'on the clouds of heaven' seems to represent the coming of Yahweh himself.[43] 'The throne of his glory', the symbol of his kingly rule, is directly mentioned later in Matthew 25:31, in the context of the eschatological judgement scene (καθίσει ἐπὶ θρόνου δόξης αὐτοῦ).

Clearly, in the Eschatological Discourse, Christology is integrated into eschatology. The future holds the coming of the one who has already come and whose 'good news of the kingdom' is proclaimed in the present (24:14). Therefore, the hope for humanity is centred on the person of Jesus, the one capable of renewing humanity and its life space, rather than on the future itself. Ultimately, the world is not moving towards chaos, though plenty of it is evident in human history (24:3-31), but rather towards Christ and the future he brings at his parousia. To that hope Matthew looks Christologically, 'with quiet but unshakeable assurance'.[44]

Vigilance and Endurance: Church, Ethics and the Eschaton

The main concern of the Eschatological Discourse is not the events marking the crisis before the eschaton, but the present existence of the church before the end. The present is a time in which affliction and proclamation take place in parallel–in such a situation the church is called to faithfully follow Christ, enduring to the end (24:13).[45] No discussion of the new world is given in Matthew 24-25, but the discourse is instead dominated by an emphasis on the ethical implications of the coming eschaton. Clearly, eschatology, discipleship and ethics are inextricably interwoven, and this link frames the discourse.[46]

This perspective is reflected in the structure of the Matthean Eschatological Discourse, as seen in the relevant section above. Namely, the shorter section on the eschatological portrayal of human history (24:3-31) functions only as

---

43 E.g. Grant Osborne, *Matthew*, ZECNT (Grand Rapids, MI: Zondervan, 2010), 894.
44 Green, *Matthew*, 49.
45 Beasley-Murray, Last Days, 352.
46 Vicky Balabanski, *Eschatology in the Making: Mark, Matthew and the Didache*, SNTSMS 97 (Cambridge: Cambridge University Press, 1997), 152. This link is characteristic to Matthew's eschatological thinking throughout the First Gospel. For the union of eschatology and ecclesiology in the Matthean discourses, see Bornkamm, *Tradition*, 15-24.

a preparation for the longer warning section (24:32-25:30) which stresses vigilance. So, the discussion on human history exists in the interest of paraenesis. This feature indicates that Matthew's primary interest lies in praxis, rather than in speculation along the lines of date-calculating imminent eschatology.[47] Thus, the readers of the discourse are to discover in it how God calls them to live in the light of the coming parousia.

The paraenetic section consists of two larger parts. First, the unexpectedness of the parousia is emphasised (24:32-44); this is followed by three parousia parables which discuss the character of waiting (24:45-25:30). The resulting picture brings out clearly that a thoughtless and careless attitude toward the parousia is to be guarded against. The congregation of disciples is rather to demonstrate watchfulness (γρηγορεῖτε οὖν; 24:42) and preparedness (γίνεσθε ἕτοιμοι; 24:44).[48] What faithfulness, readiness and responsibility in the assigned tasks in the interim period mean is illustrated by the parables of the faithful and unfaithful slave (24:45-51), the ten bridesmaids (25:1-13) and the talents (25:14-30). In these parables, the Church is urged to understand discipleship in terms of living responsibly in endurance and carrying out duties in a spiritually prepared state, since the followers of Christ do not know the time of the Son of Man's return (24:36). The warnings 'function as catalysts for the disciples' spiritual wakefulness'.[49]

The present is also seen in the Eschatological Discourse as a time of worldwide mission.[50] Bearing witness to the 'gospel of the kingdom' is directly linked to the coming of the end (24:14). As background to the idea is the motif of the nations' end-time conversion to the Lord which features prominently in the Old Testament prophetic literature.[51] Though in the Greek future passive construction of 24:14 the subject of the preaching is not specified (κηρυχθήσεται ['will be proclaimed']), the context indicates that those who endure the trials delineated in the discourse are precisely those who persevere until the end, faithfully bearing witness to 'the gospel of the kingdom'. In the wider context of the

---

47   Luz, *Matthew*, 3:203.
48   Rabbi Zera claims that three come when the mind is diverted: the messiah, a found article, and a scorpion (b. Sanh. 97a).
49   Talbert, *Matthew*, 278.
50   This emphasis is typical to the post-Easter period: e.g. Acts 1:8. Since in Matt 24:14 the post-Easter period is in view, there is no contradiction with 10:5-6.
51   E.g. Isa 2:2-4; 45:20-22; 49:6; 55:5; 56:6-8; Mic 4:1-3; cf. 1 En. 48:4-5; T. Levi 18:5-9; Sib. Or. 3:710-723.

entire Gospel, this missionary task is clearly given to the church and it has an eschatological overtone (28:19-20). As demonstrated, church, ethics and eschatology are strongly linked in the theological horizon of the Eschatological Discourse: none ranks above the others, but they are all integral to the realisation of the pastoral purpose of the author.

The Only Task that Matters: Serving While Waiting

While the Eschatological Discourse alerts its audience to the time of crisis in the post-Easter era and emphasises the triumph of God's plan, its aim is not to inspire a short-term eschatological fervour. On the one hand, the discourse communicates important information about the end-time, listing many of the signs that marked the end in contemporary Jewish literature.[52] Although these prophecies make the suffering of the people of God bearable, they are, however, not of cardinal significance. The exhortative nature of the discourse makes of focal interest the instruction on how to live in the light of the impending parousia. So, the invitation to the disciples is not so much to discern the future, but rather the present.[53] This practically means that the expectation of the parousia does not entail any passivity in the life of the believing community, but rather it requires a careful and dedicated activity in the service of God. This perspective is emphatically reinforced in the concluding scene of the discourse, the parable of the sheep and the goats, which portrays the universal judgement scene taking place in front of (ἔμπροσθεν; 25:32) 'the throne of his glory' (θρόνος δόξης αὐτοῦ; 25:31). The significance of the location is in highlighting the divine authority in serving cosmic justice.

The point of the universal judgement scene (25:31-46) is to emphasise the criterion used at the last judgment. The characteristic of 'the righteous' (οἱ δίκαιοι) is that they give food to the hungry, give something to drink to the thirsty, welcome strangers, clothe the naked, take care of the sick and visit those in prison (25:35-45). The concept of demonstrating mercy to 'the least of these'

---

52 Craig S. Keener (*The Gospel of Matthew: A Socio-Rhetorical Commentary* [Grand Rapids, MI: Eerdmans, 2009], 566 n. 104) lists the following Jewish sources: Jub. 23:11-25; 1QM 15:1; Sib. Or. 2:6-3:33; 3:213-215; 4 Ezra 8:63-9:8; 13:19-20, 30; 2 Bar. 26:1-27:13; 69:3-5; T. Mos. 7-8; m. Sota 9:15; b. Sanh. 97a; Pesiq. Rab Kah. 5:9; Qoh. Rab. 2:15 §2; Lam. Rab. 1:13, §41; Song Rab. 2:13 §4; 8:9, §3; Pesiq. R. 1:7; 15:14/15; 34:1.
53 Hauerwas, Matthew, 206.

(25:40, 45) reminds us of Proverbs 19:17: 'Whoever is kind to the poor lends to the Lord, and will be repaid in full.' What is new in Matthew 25 is not the idea of mercy (cf. 5:7), but the identification of the needy person with Jesus himself. According to the judgement scene, Christian piety is directly linked with the love commandment: serving God takes place when acts of love are extended towards other human beings, including one's enemies.[54] Vine notes that 'this is not a self-imposed status'[55]–acts of love are rather marked by a genuine, warm fraternity which becomes an extension of the messianic era of shalom. At the end, it seems that this is 'the only crisis that matters',[56] the way to remain awake in waiting for the fulfilment of the promise of the glorious second coming.

Conclusion

The theology of the Matthean Eschatological Discourse is a pastoral theology: its primary concern is to guide the community of believers. The author incarnates crucial moral imperatives by setting up a complex interplay of eschatology, judgement theology, philosophy of history, Christology, ecclesiology and ethics.

Instead of an extended speculation on the question of 'the sign' of his coming (24:3), the Matthean Jesus discusses with his disciples how they are to wait in the era between the two advents. Unfortunately, Christians have often been unable to heed Jesus' warning. They have often made apocalyptic constructs on the basis of the Eschatological Discourse, attempting to determine the end of the age and doing exactly what Jesus warned against: stepping on the territory of the knowledge reserved for the Father only (24:36). The recent Covid-19 pandemic and the Ukrainian-Russian conflict have provided ample evidence of that.

This essay has argued that Jesus' use of apocalyptic language in Matthew 24-25, despite its strong judgement theology, is not given for speculation over the future, but rather for ethical-ecclesial purposes: to help the disciples to live attentively and responsibly in the presence of the one who has come and who will come. As such, the discourse helps us to see ourselves and the world in which we are called to live in the light of God's purposes for his creation. While

---

54 I. Howard Marshall, *New Testament Theology* (Downers Grove, IL: InterVarsity, 2004), 110.
55 Vine, *Jesus*, 52.
56 Hauerwas, *Matthew*, 212.

the discourse undeniably calls attention prophetically to the challenges the followers of Christ face between the two advents, focusing on reading 'the signs of the times' does not do justice to Jesus' teaching which seeks to instruct on how to live in the light of the coming parousia.

The challenge the church of the 21st century is facing is to bring the study of the Eschatological Discourse out from a purely academic realm into the concerns of everyday life. Our age strongly resonates with apocalyptic dystopia as far as human history is concerned, but this is only part of the story. Our generation has the privilege of learning to recognise and embrace the 'seeds of hope'[57] sown with intentionality in the Eschatological Discourse. The church is tasked with carrying forward these 'seeds of hope' as 'this good news of the kingdom' (24:14) in the conviction that God is at work through the processes of human history and that he will complete his job of restoration in his own time. According to the Eschatological Discourse, such a perspective will materialise in an attitude of watchful expectation of the future that will be brought about by the eschatological intervention of God which goes hand in hand with service to those in need.

---

57 An expression taken from Henri Nouwen (*Seeds of Hope*, ed. Robert Durback [London: Darton, Longman & Todd, 1989]).

Part 2
Reflective Perspectives

The Right Thing to Do
A Reflection on Navigating the Complexities of Everyday Moral Choices

Michael Pearson

My first recollection of meeting Gunnar Pedersen is of him attending meetings of the Newbold College Board of Governors. Among all the soberly suited Board members, Gunnar stood out, dressed as he was in a black leather jacket and roll-neck sweater. There was a freshness about him and a quiet thoughtfulness which drew my attention. When later he became head of the Department of Theological Studies, he gave his colleagues the freedom to teach as we saw fit without any intrusion. I will try to offer something here in the same spirit of openness.

What Ought I to Do?

Most people, whether they know it or not, engage in ethical and philosophical conversation every day of their lives. The questions may often be simple but they are nonetheless serious. They ask: 'In the present situation, what is the right thing to do? What ought I to do?' Paying a fare or the cost of an item when you could get away with not paying, would be an example. Telling the truth in everyday conversation where the truth might be awkward or upsetting, would be another. Or they will freely volunteer an opinion on some moral or social matter of the day. If we are going to engage in this important activity often if not daily, it is important that we do it well. That is what ethics is about. In the present circumstance, what is the right thing to do? Basically, it is very simple.

But it is also true that such conversations can get very complex, for it is mostly the case that there are so many factors to consider. People can become bewildered and may look for simple answers to relieve them of the burden of thinking the problem through, and perhaps admitting some responsibility. We should always be wary of such oversimplifications and people who offer them. It is usually an attempt at evading our responsibility to engage with things which challenge us. And lazy over-simplifications can harm people.

A Method

There is much to set your head spinning in our world. Modern technology with its endless possibilities, the speed of communication, the mix of the world's populations, medical innovation, the struggle for power, limited resources for infinite need and so much more. I used to find students sometimes became perplexed by problems which were thrown up by open conversation about the sorts of dilemmas they would find in ministry or in their secular workplace. There were the more obvious issues of the day such as divorce, abortion, same-sex relations and changing gender roles. The Church at that time would mostly avoid such difficult subjects, provide answers which operated simply at the level of policy, or provide a lowest common denominator response.

But there were many other issues beyond the grand themes which were thrown up by everyday life in the Church which were just as distressing. As the students' guide through such problems, I wanted to find some way of approaching such issues which provided clarity along with honesty, and which at the same time honoured the Adventist tradition. But I have always been suspicious of any attempt to produce tight theoretical structures when it comes to our understanding of God and his people. There is the real danger that you seek to fit the Living God and vibrant human beings into your own template, and inevitably distort everything.

Nevertheless, I did evolve a method which was basically very simple and offered some security while allowing freedom of thought. It tried to do justice to the richness of human individuality but also recognised the centrality of community. It offered some order, some sense of knowing where you are while providing freedom to roam around within those parameters. Students needed some sort of sense of where the boundaries were.

What follows is a simplified version of that approach. For the purposes of this essay, I will use 'ethical' and 'moral' interchangeably, though I understand important distinctions can be made.

The Matrix

The concept of the matrix does not offer definitive answers, but it does offer a structure within which mature answers to difficult questions may be faithfully sought.

Imagine a square.

Place within it a question such as 'Is it ever justified to tell a lie?' Any moral question will fit into the centre of the square.

Bring to bear on the question four of the main ways in which thinkers over the centuries have tried to approach such moral questions.

On one side of the square is Authority. All our decisions are made within some framework of authority and rules. These may be the laws of a country, the rules of an institution, the traditions of a community, the teachings of a charismatic leader, a sacred text and so on.

On another side is Consequence. When we make decisions, we frequently calculate likely outcomes, desirable or undesirable.

On the third side is Virtue and this is perhaps more difficult to grasp. What would a virtuous person do? How would a virtuous person seek to flourish via the choice they will make in the present circumstance?

Lastly there is Story. When we make decisions, we will frequently have a story in the back of our minds which in some way bears on the present dilemma. Jesus understood this very well in his use of parables. All communities have their stories. The story could be a biblical narrative such as the Good Samaritan but equally could be a Greek myth, or the life of a contemporary celebrity, the experience of a friend or relative, a folk legend or a famous episode in history.

What do a consideration of authority, consequences, virtue and narrative bring to our dilemma?

It is important to insist that this method will not solve our dilemma. But it will offer us some understanding of the breadth of the problem, and what must be taken into consideration if a mature judgement is to be made. Too often our moral judgements are made from a very confined and subjective point of view.

And there is no getting away from it: in the end it is we who must make a judgement. No-one else, no system can do that for us if we are to live into our full humanity. We must make a judgement, a choice, and ultimately accept responsibility for it. So often people seek to avoid the burden of choosing by simply appealing to an authority.

Let us look at each of these sides of the square more closely.

Authority, Rules: Deontology

If you are seeking a response to a moral dilemma, a reasonable place to start is to ask what the rules say. This appeal to rules is technically called deontology. The authority might be state laws, the regulations of a particular community, the Ten Commandments, the words of a charismatic leader and so on. It could also be natural law, that is when people tend to say, 'It's not natural' , as with the transplantation of animal organs into humans, or cross-dressing.

Such rules are important and may help to make life simple and secure, but they may also make it rigid and leave us unable to respond to the infinite complexities of everyday life. Almost all rules admit of exceptions, so it becomes important to know when it is appropriate to over-ride a rule. A biblical example of this perhaps is when Jesus says: 'You have heard it said ... but I say unto you ...' You need to know about the authority of the rule-giver and whether you trust that authority. Untold numbers of people have suffered because an authority figure–a father, a priest, a dictator–has not recognised the need to nuance a rule, to admit an exception, to exercise mercy.

And people may do the right thing but for quite the wrong reason. Or maybe the authority does not cover the case in point. An appeal to authority may be necessary but is not usually sufficient to resolve the dilemma.[1]

Consequences, Outcomes: Consequentialism

When we choose option A rather than B or C, we frequently judge which will provide the most satisfactory outcome from our point of view. This may mean that we bypass authority for the time being.

We use this approach to moral questions at least as much as we invoke authority. And it is essential to do so. But we can only calculate likely outcomes of our actions. We often cannot be certain. We are sometimes wrong in our predictions. We must ask questions about precisely who sees this as the best outcome. Is it in the interests of the majority, a particular minority, your group or just you? Do we consider long-term outcomes along with short-term ones? Is it legitimate to arrive at a desired outcome via oppressive means? Much human suffering has been inflicted on others by those who believed that their present violence would eventually produce the greatest happiness for the majority.[2]

Living Well, Flourishing: Virtue Ethics

This third approach is probably the most difficult to grasp. Indeed, scholars have produced a variety of understandings of it, and this is simply mine. Suffice it to say that it is about choosing courses of moral action which will permit the individual to flourish as a human being, flourishing being understood in a broad context. It is also important to note that my flourishing cannot be achieved at your expense. A virtuous person will consider the well-being, the prospering of the whole community of interest, though they will not necessarily be able to satisfy all its demands. Virtue is in the same broad family as the state of blessedness described in the first psalm. The blessed 'are like trees planted by a stream of water, which yield their fruit in its season, and their leaves do not wither. In

---

1 See Robin Gill, ed., *The Cambridge Companion to Christian Ethics* (Cambridge: Cambridge University Press, 2001).

2 See Katarzyna De Lazari-Radek and Peter Singer, *Utilitarianism: A Very Short Introduction* (Oxford: Oxford University Press, 2017).

all that they do they prosper.' There is something secure about this blessedness because the tree is next to the life-giving source of water. There is something measured, ordered and appropriate about the tree which produces 'fruit in due season'. A consideration of virtue offers an important but not straightforward approach to moral issues.[3]

Stories, Heroes: Narrative Ethics

It is not unusual for us to look for a familiar story to enlighten us as we confront a tricky moral decision. If we are Christian, we are likely to go to a biblical narrative. If we were ancient Greeks, we would have gone to one of the myths, which are still very much in circulation today. Many people today look to celebrities or folk heroes. We may simply refer to family and friends for a guiding story: 'Well my cousin faced the same problem and she ...' Such stories can not only inform but also inspire in us capacities which we may need to confront our own dilemma. We can make such stories work for us as we find our way through a testing time. There are of course problems with this looking for such precedents too. Is the story sufficiently close to the present problem to be a reliable guide? How do I choose a single story among the many I know? Do I choose only one which casts me in a good light or offers me a good role? Nevertheless, this is a common way in which we find our way through our present difficulties. All societies have their folklore and charismatic figures who offer a light in the darkness.[4]

Using the Matrix

These are of course simplifications of moral theories, and some would want to add others or modify these. The matrix was designed for students going into ministry or another vocation, for student groups of mixed ability, and was to be taught within certain time constraints. That said, it does encourage students to work with sometimes uncomfortable levels of moral complexity.

---

[3] See Alasdair MacIntyre, *After Virtue: A Study in Moral Theory* (London: Bloomsbury, 2014) and Tom Wright, *Virtue Reborn* (London: SPCK, 2010).
[4] See Jakob Lothe and Jeremy Hawthorn, eds., *Narrative Ethics* (Amsterdam: Rodopi, 2013).

It is our job to apply the approaches raised on all sides of the square to the question in the centre. Some of the considerations will pull in different directions inevitably. Some people will weigh different evidence differently. Different people may consider the same factors and finally come to a different conclusion. We have to weigh the merits of each as we might weigh two different objects, say a book and a bottle of water, in either hand, and judge which is the heavier. We may appear to make a simple judgement but in fact hundreds of messages will be going between brain, arm and hand as we do so. So it is with moral decisions. Then finally we must commit ourselves to a judgement and live with it. It is not an easy business but then life is not easy.

None of the answers will be perfect. Beware of simple solutions. In most cases they are not available, though there will be pressure to say that they are. The matrix enables us to enter into a conversation about an issue as opposed to blind opting.

Example: Military Service in Ukraine

It may help to examine an example. Let us consider the plight of a young Ukrainian person who is a Christian, wondering whether to take up arms as some of his/her friends are urging him to do. He sees what is happening in his country today and must decide whether to take up arms to oppose the aggressor.

Authority: First he must consider those people or traditions which he regards as having some authority over him. He has heard the elected government's calls to arms. He believes that his country is a legitimately established nation state to which he owes some loyalty. It seems to him that this struggle satisfies the conditions of a 'just war' against a perpetrator who is inflicting grievous wounds on his fellow countrymen and even perhaps on some he loves. He believes there is a moral obligation to protect human dignity and freedom.

At the same time the biblical commandment tells him 'You shall not kill' or perhaps 'murder'. Yet in the Old Testament he reads of various atrocities committed in the name of God to protect Israel. More than that, he follows Jesus who refused to take up arms in pursuit of the kingdom, who refused to sanction guerrilla warfare against the vicious occupying Roman force. Jesus yielded himself to state violence rather than become the aggressor. His kingdom was not to be built on the exercise of brute power.

And what does his own Church community say? It says that you must, if at all possible, avoid hostilities, even perhaps while supporting the national effort by providing medical aid, ensuring food supplies get through, keeping energy supplies functioning. Non-combatancy may be compatible with faithfulness to the values for which your society stands. But in the end the advice from the Church is to follow your own conscience.

Consequentialism: If this young person fights for his country, he will be seeking to ensure the safety and security of his fellow-countrymen not just for now but for generations. More than that he understands that Ukraine is fighting a war on behalf of many millions beyond his own country. Millions in Europe and beyond will benefit from his efforts. The use of force is regrettable but necessary in the present extreme circumstances. But he wants to stay safe. He fears the privations of military service. He must think of his family, his ageing parents who depend on his support in many ways. What would they do without him? And then there is the inevitable carnage which he will involve himself in. Is it possible for him to know where this slippery slope will lead?

Virtue: He must consider how he and his compatriots will best flourish as human beings. Will it be as citizens of Europe or as subjects in an enlarged ancient Mother Russia? Where will he be truly 'blessed' not simply at the economic level? Is the hope of an honest and open society enough to make him fight for it? Is he willing simply to bend to the invading force with who knows what consequences? Could he really 'live well' on the front line? Could he live well afterwards knowing that others—some of his friends perhaps—have sacrificed their lives for the greater good while he stayed safe? Would guilt cloud all his days?

Narrative: There are so many narratives being offered in all the media, and also in the churches. Who really is the aggressor? Is this a 'war' or just a limited 'special military operation'? Are both sides guilty of similar atrocities? Are NATO or the USA really seeking world domination? Is this one man's war? Is there some truth in the story of Mother Russia slowly weakened by the decadent west? Is Ukraine merely the fall guy for countries who will not risk open engagement? For how long has Ukraine been a sovereign nation anyway? The national boundaries in that part of the world have always been somewhat fluid. Some in his Church may warn that in such dire circumstances there can be no 'winners'.

The Matrix at Work

The matrix will show the student where the evidence may lie. It does not provide them with its precise location. It is the moral responsibility of the student to seek the evidence in a way which covers as many angles as possible. But, of course, the angles are numerous, and some may be overlooked. That is the risk of making your own choices. You choose and have to bear the responsibility for so doing.

As suggested above, it is like deciding which is the heavier of two unlike objects in your hands. As you think about it, multiple areas of your nervous system are sending relevant information to your brain to process. It may be a close call but in the end you may opt for a carton of milk on the basis of what your neural system is telling you. But it might just be the book.

So it is with ethical decision-making.

If you are a Christian, then you will ascribe a particular weight to the authority of the Scriptures–especially perhaps the words of Jesus. But then the Bible does not address many of the dilemmas which face us today though there may be relevant principles. You will consider what your Church community says. You will listen to the views of trusted family and friends. You will read reliable commentators.

But it must be admitted that when faced with such difficult questions we will probably have an instinctive response, a 'gut feeling'. This must be consulted because it probably represents a wisdom accumulated over the years. But this wisdom may be skewed, and it is probably the main function of the matrix to correct and balance such an instinctive response. The matrix will encourage us to visit some places for guidance which we have not visited before.

There are so many people and organisations out there who seek to shape our view that we need some support to shape our ideas. The alternative is that many will rush into the arms of some strong man or woman who seems to offer security in the chaos.

Students would sometimes ask me for my own opinion about a particular case or issue. My reply frequently was that my own opinion really did not matter very much. They were not to regard me as some sort of oracle. However, I would add that I would provide them with my response accompanied by my reasons when we as a group had finished debating the question. I would also often present them with a specific case and ask them to work with it with the matrix as a support and prompt in their search.

The matrix achieved two things. First, it gave them the security of a framework within which to work. Second it offered them the freedom to think for themselves about the issue. I wanted them to learn to think for themselves. It was after all what they would have to do when they left the relative safety of the College environment. Some were uncomfortable about this approach; others said that they had learnt how to think clearly as a result. They had come from different backgrounds and with different gifts, and I suppose that both reactions were natural.

A More Important Question

I suggested at the outset that the central question in ethics is 'What ought I to do?' But there is a still more fundamental question to be asked by anyone claiming to be a follower of Jesus. And I think it applies beyond the Christian community, though not all would agree. That cardinal question is: 'Who am I?' Who am I becoming?' 'Who do I wish to become?' Three facets of the same question. While the original question is about doing–what should I do?–this is about being–who am I? Our actions issue from who, in the deepest place, we are. The response to the question 'What should I do?' issues out of our response to the question 'Who am I? Who am I becoming?' And responding to that is the work of a lifetime.

Conclusion

I always regarded my work in ethics classes as essentially helping to form truly human beings–not transmitting facts or even supplying right answers. This work involves students slowly becoming wise. That means a readiness to grow beyond traditional formulae and present boundaries. It may mean encountering a daunting moment of clarity, a Damascus Road revelation perhaps. At such times we need a friend to support us. It was my job to be that friend, willing to tell hard truths if necessary, ready to provide support when the scaffolding of life was dismantled.

It means recognising that authority systems eventually run out of road. They have no more to say to us. That can be a frightening place to be. At such times we need to have a community which will sustain us in its wisdom. We need people in that community who show us generosity of spirit and who allow us to be confused or angry or sceptical for a while.

As we face such complex challenges, personal or universal, we stand in need of a certain grace and welcome if we are not to be overwhelmed. That is what Christian community is about. Gunnar knew that very well.

In His Will Is Our Peace

Radisa Antic

Even the greatest scientists have noticed, having completed their work, that science, regardless of how proud it is of its own victories and achievements, remains powerless to satisfy the deepest needs of our being. Undeniably, life's events together with the exhausting round of daily concerns often prevent us from making time for the fruitful contemplation of the meaning of life, and scaling the heights where religious truths shimmer.

However, the birth of a child, the family that we have founded, death that looms all around us (sometimes we only narrowly avoid it), extreme misfortunes, incurable illnesses, all draw the attention of even the simplest people to the essential questions of human destiny. The almost inaudible whisper of an old woman, on her knees in some village church, reflects the same lack of knowledge, the same feeling of unfathomableness, as the intellectual explorations of the scientist or the emotional eruptions of the poet. Whatever our circumstances, we are all equal, thirsty for certainty and security, restless and bewildered the moment that we trip on a rock, when we face an obstacle or when we are injured by thorns on our path to eternity.

Man's Spiritual Thirst

Who am I and why am I here? Are we alone in the universe? What are my aspirations and my hopes? What will happen when I die? Any person who is at all spiritually minded, asks himself/herself these questions sooner or later. Some choose to study theology and philosophy, usually not for any materialistic reasons, but with the desire to resolve their own life's dilemmas. It is difficult to say to what extent they are successful in this. However, they certainly gain some answers that will help them improve their daily lives and give them meaning.

Petar II Petrović Njegoš, the great Montenegrin author and bishop, contracted tuberculosis early in life and died very young, at the age of 38. His literary opus includes the Testament in which, among other things, Njegoš describes how his last moments will pass, what his funeral will be like, how the Montenegrins will react to the death of the young bishop. Some extremely moving lines are dedicated to his father Tomo. In them Njegoš recalls how his father had seen him off many times: off to school, off on different journeys, but the send-off that was inevitably coming would be special in every way. It would be the last send-off.[1]

Similar to this, there are last, final questions in life, questions of everlasting importance. In these turbulent times of ours the world has been engulfed in a serious crisis and it is no longer such a comfortable place where people can live peacefully. We find some of the answers in the Bible. According to one author,[2] there is only one book while all others stem from it or flow into it. One of its old texts, Ecclesiastes, speaks of the human thirst which no stream of water in this world can quench.

Chapter 6 of Ecclesiastes

The text of Ecclesiastes was written around 940 BCE, which means that almost 3,000 years separate us from its appearance. However, in a way it is very contemporary since it helps us understand our personal needs and the problems that we face. In the Hebrew Bible the book is called תֹהֶלֶת (*qoheleth*), whereas in English it is *Ecclesiastes*, which is the Greek translation of the Hebrew expression. The word תֹהֶלֶת is derived from another Hebrew word, קָהָל, which designated the church in the Old Testament. *Qoheleth* is the teacher, someone who taught people in church. And it is precisely a *qoheleth* who wrote the book in question here. One could say without any exaggeration that it has inspired many authors, probably Tolstoy and Dostoyevsky, perhaps the philosophers Schopenhauer and

---

1 Petar Petrovic Njegos, *Testamenat* (Podgorica: Istocnik, 2003), 29.
2 Matija Bećković, 'Odgovori Na Sva Pitanja Su u Jednoj Knjizi, Bibliji', *Novosti Plus*, February 2003, 12.

Nietzsche, and even more recent authors, such as Sartre and Camus. All of them drew their inspiration in one way or another from Ecclesiastes.

In his book the Preacher speaks about thirst, the human thirst that no horizontal reality can quench. It is believed that the book was written by Solomon, who is considered the wisest of men, but we should also keep in mind that it is the Word of God.

The sixth chapter of *Ecclesiastes* starts with the words, 'I have seen another evil under the sun.' Here the Hebrew text alludes to a very great evil. Previously mentioned are different evils that humanity faces here on Earth, and in the sixth chapter the writer speaks of one that is even greater than the rest. The Hebrew text points out: 'I have seen another evil, and it *weighs heavily* on men.' You have the impression that this is like a sack of sand that we are forced to carry.

As a comparison, let us take a look at the evils that are mentioned in the previous chapters. The fourth chapter states, 'Again I looked and saw all the oppression that was taking place under the sun: I saw the tears of the oppressed, and they have no comforter; power was on the side of their oppressors.' This is a very modern thought. Look at today's young people who are angrily protesting across the planet, and who revolt because they have no work, and no prospects. Solomon also speaks of the economically oppressed, who unfortunately could not do anything because power was in the hands of their masters.

Another evil follows in the fourth verse: 'And I saw that all labour and all achievement spring from man's envy of his neighbour'–a well-known problem, also typical of today. This is madness, Solomon says, an evil that destroys the one who feeds it. The third evil listed in the fourth chapter is loneliness, which is also a present-day phenomenon. Millions of people worldwide feel lonely, even though they almost always live in an anthill. People are alone both in their family and in society. Solomon further explains why loneliness is evil. He says that two are better than one because they will earn more, or 'if one falls down, his friend can help him up'; then, in the case of an attack two will more easily defend themselves, and if it is cold, they will be warmer. It is interesting that 940 years before Christ, Solomon spoke about loneliness, which is so widespread in society today. The fifth chapter goes on to address the issues of oppression, futility of effort and the transience of everything.

It has previously been mentioned that the sixth chapter speaks of an evil that is different from these just listed, one much graver, and one that weighs heavily on humanity, and for which there is no human solution. Solomon does not reveal its nature at first, but through careful reading it is possible to unravel it. The second verse says, 'God gives a man wealth, possessions and honour, so that he lacks nothing his heart desires', pointing out the fact that everything we have is a gift from God. So, everything would be wonderful if there were not a 'yet' following it. 'But God does not enable him to enjoy them, and a stranger enjoys them instead. This is meaningless, a grievous evil.'

So, you may have all the riches in the world, all the honour in the world, but if you lack this one dimension, something that only God can give you, then in Solomon's words, this is 'grievous evil'–even more so since someone else later enjoys it. There are different commentaries on this text, which is quite probably autobiographical. In fact, after Solomon's death, it was not his son who took the throne, but a stranger. This is also happening today, when millionaires worldwide have no one to leave their fortunes to, and then they are often inherited by strangers.

In the third verse Solomon continues his thought: 'A man may have a hundred children'. Most people today believe that in a way they can continue to live in their children, through their children. This too is true. Children do in fact bring immense joy and great happiness to their parents. However, it is also true that children can be the source of great difficulties in the family. This is why when Solomon says, 'If a man fathers a hundred children and lives many years ... but his soul is not satisfied with life's good things', we still do not know what is missing.

So, we may have honour and wealth, we may live many years, we may have a hundred children, but if something is missing, some of God's 'spice' , then 'a stillborn child is better off than he' . Once again this is an historical fact. If you have read the Bible, perhaps you remember that a child was born from the illegitimate relationship between David and Bathsheba, the wife of Uriah the Hittite, but the child died immediately after birth. David would later marry Bathsheba and they would have a son, Solomon.

Further in the text the Preacher emphasises the following: 'It comes without meaning, it departs in darkness, and in darkness its name is shrouded.' Often in his book he analyses human existence: before birth we are in darkness, when we see the light of day, we start to live (the light is simply life), and in the end we return to darkness. Therefore, everything is in vain unless there is something to fill this void.

Just remember some of the most influential intellectuals of the twentieth century, such as Sartre, who left an indelible mark on European thinking, or Albert Camus, who was intellectually close to him, even though they never met or collaborated. Both claimed that life is plain absurdity. Sartre said that if we investigate the past, I am not there. Between me today and me in the past there is nothingness because I am not what I used to be in the past; I am now a different person.[3] Apparent here is Heraclitus' influence and his claim that 'everything flows'.

Or, as Sartre continues, if we look into the future, I will not be there either, because between me today and me in the future there is nothingness; I will not be the same person in the future.[4] This is a direct allusion to Heraclitus's thought that you cannot step twice into the same stream since everything is moving and changing. Or you never return to the same home since it is older, and you are older. And the same goes for friends. So, this is the tragic fact that thinkers correctly noticed: the movement and transience of human reality.

Therefore, Sartre claimed that human existence is absurd and that the only purpose of human existence is precisely to accept this absurdity, to accept the fact that there is no purpose. This was the message of the secular twentieth-century existentialists. There are also, incidentally, Christian existentialists, such as Dostoyevsky and Kierkegaard.

Let us go back to Solomon's argument. 'Even if he lives a thousand years twice over' , if we lack the most important element of human existence, everything is in vain yet again. However, according to Solomon, even two thousand years would not solve the problem. The following, seventh, verse emphasises a very important truth: 'All man's efforts are for his mouth, yet his appetite is never satisfied.' The English translation of the Bible states that the 'appetite' can never be satisfied. The Hebrew text uses the word נֶפֶשׁ, soul. Perceived in this light, this verse gains a much deeper meaning: all of mankind's efforts are often reduced to

---

3   Donald Palmer, *Looking at Philosophy* (Mountain View, CA: Mayfield Publishing Company, 1988), 367.
4   Donald Palmer, *Looking at Philosophy*, 367.

satisfying purely physical needs, which cannot fulfil what is spiritual within us, to achieve the supreme good. A similar sense is contained in the seventh verse of the book's first chapter, which states that 'all streams flow into the sea, yet the sea is never full'. Perhaps then one might say that all the streams of this world cannot quench the thirst of the human soul if it lacks this still unknown ingredient. Later, in the ninth verse, we find that the human soul seems to be wandering and looking for something. This is certainly not a soul separated from the body; it is not dualism. This is an essential need of the human being, its deepest need.

Let us summarise the message of the entire sixth chapter. The wise Solomon seems to be shouting to human beings saying: 'People, I want to tell you something. You can have treasures, honour, live many years, even live a thousand years twice over, you may have a hundred children, but if you lack what is most important–then everything is in vain.' Of course, many would not agree with this. However, in his search Nietzsche reveals that 'something' to us.[5] Despite being an atheist, Nietzsche deserves our attention because of his sincerity and passionate desire to understand the world. During his lifetime Germany experienced great progress, but he said this was not what was most important. He was born during the industrial revolution and during a period of great scientific progress, but he claimed that this was not the most important thing. Then he added something very interesting: On all the walls of this world, wherever they may exist, I will write one and the same question–does God exist or not? Unfortunately, he believed that God does not exist. We will not agree with him on this issue, but one should point out his idea that there is something far more important than economic problems, although according to Marx, the economy is very important. There is something more important in man's life and Nietzsche, one of the most lucid thinkers of all time, paves the way towards this thought. Finally, what is that which is missing, what is this thirst that all the streams of this world cannot quench? The Bible is truly the most authoritative source to offer us the right answer.

---

5 See Hans Küng, *Does God Exist? An Answer for Today* (Garden City, NY: Doubleday, 1980), 372.

At Jacob's Well

The text in Ecclesiastes is not the only one to discuss the thirst of the human soul. The most famous verses on this topic are in the fourth chapter of the Gospel of John, which describes the encounter of Jesus Christ with a Samaritan woman. This is the conversation immortalised on painters' canvases and is well known in the history of Christianity. In the thirteenth verse of this chapter Jesus says: 'Everyone who drinks this water will be thirsty again, but whoever drinks the water I give him will never thirst.' To superficial people these words seem incomprehensible and mysterious. As Jesus spoke these words, he pointed to Jacob's Well where women went to fetch water, usually early in the morning or late in the evening. The woman in question here appeared at the well at noon, to avoid probing eyes and unpleasant questions, since she had five failed marriages behind her. During the history of Christianity, the name of this woman has often been uttered in a negative tone. However, in recent years people have started thinking differently about the Samaritan woman. In Jesus Christ's time it was not the woman who searched for a husband, but rather the man who chose a wife. Therefore, the Samaritan woman changed hands, like a commodity, from one master to the next. A total of five failed marriages! And it often takes only one to destroy a person's life! That is why in the city of Sychar, whose name means city of drunk people, no one wanted to socialise with such a woman, which is clearly why she felt very lonely. While she was fetching water, Jesus Christ appeared and started to talk to her about the great truth that also preoccupied Solomon. The water from earthly springs can only temporarily quench thirst. Since in the Bible water symbolizes life, *the water that Jesus offered was indicative of eternity, of eternal life*. If you follow the text, you will note that while Jesus spoke about eternal values, the Samaritan woman was constantly thinking of earthly, material water. In the beginning it was difficult for her to understand what Jesus was trying to teach her. The most important message of the Holy Scriptures is that although we have about seventy or eighty years in this world, we were not created to die, that God who gives the gift of wealth, honours, children, can also provide water which will satisfy our deepest needs; he can give us life. In other words, human existence can only have meaning if there is eternity.

If life is reduced solely to our brief worldly journey, then it is very difficult to avoid Sartre's and Camus' conclusion that life is absurd, that life is a torment, and that the only meaning of human existence is precisely to accept that there is no meaning.

The Thirst Can in Fact be Quenched

In his Epistle to the Hebrews, Paul gives his famous definition of faith: 'Now faith is confidence in what we hope for' (Heb 11:1). What we are hoping for is the meaningful end to human history, i.e. Christ's second coming. But Paul also adds 'and assurance about what we do not see'. The Greek οὐ βλεπομένων, which means 'that which cannot be seen', applies to creation. In other words, the entire Christian perception of the world shows that the history of mankind has a meaningful beginning, i.e. the creation of the world, and that it has a meaningful end. However, there are problems, there are tsunamis, there are 'Auschwitzes', there are illnesses, and there are tragedies. However, there is also harmony in this world. Gottfried Leibnitz, renowned for his optimism, advocated the principle of sufficient reason, according to which no fact could be considered truthful or existing, nor could a single truthful statement be found without containing sufficient explanation why it is so and not any other way.[6]

We can also put it this way: there are so many miracles within ourselves and all around us, but God does not leave us without an answer. Christianity is not an irrational religion; there are things that we cannot understand, but there are also those that we are completely capable of comprehending.

Consequently, the thirst of the human soul, which cannot be quenched by all the streams of this world, can be quenched by God's message that there is something more than this life, that there is eternal life. In verse twelve of the sixth chapter of Ecclesiastes, Solomon asks: 'For who knows what is good for a man in life?' This is a rhetorical question, and the Hebrew word טוֹב, 'good', which is one of the crucial words at the beginning of the Bible, alludes to the creation when everything was very good. And then he continues: 'Who can tell him what will happen under the sun after he is gone?' Again, there are these two dimensions.

If you have the strength to believe that human life was created by chance, then that which Solomon speaks of is absurd. And indeed, there are people

---

[6] See Donal Palmer, *Looking at Philosophy*, 170 and 171.

among the world's outstanding intellectuals, even among university professors, who even though they believe in the Holy Scriptures, accept the theory of evolution, without going any deeper into this subject, and solely because leading international scientists claim evolution trumps Divine creation as recorded in the Scriptures. However, if there is a meaningful beginning and a meaningful end, then human life is not meaningless. Meaning exists, the principle of sufficient reason or internal harmony, which Leibnitz spoke of, also exists.

'In His Will is Our Peace'

If somewhere deep inside your soul you feel a thirst for something that exceeds ordinary life, be assured that such a thirst can only be satisfied by God. A well-known English author expressed this in the following way:

> Creatures are not born with desires unless satisfaction for those desires exists. A baby feels hunger: well, there is such a thing as food. A duckling wants to swim: well, there is such a thing as water. Men feel sexual desire: well, there is such a thing as sex. If I find in myself a desire which no experience in this world can satisfy, the most probable explanation is that I was made for another world.[7]

How foreign is death to us, this darkness into which we finally depart. We all want to live. If there is no satisfying this desire, then we are certainly created for some other world where there is no death. It is quite reasonable that mankind, engulfed in daily needs and illnesses, can hardly think about that which is eternal. However, the essence of the Bible is to teach people that eternity exists, that there is a God who is the source of life, that *death does not have the final word.*

It is also said that the evils mentioned at the start of Ecclesiastes, the evil of oppression, the evil of loneliness and envy, can be overcome in some way. In the case of oppression, some propose revolution. We rid ourselves of loneliness if we seek out a friend. However, the evil that Solomon speaks of in the sixth chapter of Ecclesiastes has nothing in common with what we do or do not have, but has to do with what we are, who we are as people. And as humans we stand with one

---

[7] C. S. Lewis, *Mere Christianity* (London: Harper Collins: 1952), 23.

foot in the physiological world. We feel hunger, thirst, we have other physiological needs and therefore we are limited. However, with the other foot we stand in the spiritual world, which many intellectual people have understood. We can exceed ourselves. Human thought transcends everything. Some have asked how it is possible that in Auschwitz, where there were thousands of dead every day, people still wrote love poems, or people dying of starvation shared their piece of bread with a neighbour. If we are solely motivated by the struggle for survival, it is impossible to explain any noble urges. Therefore, even though we are physiological beings, we transcend ourselves and our limitations, encouraged by our need for eternity, for the living water that Jesus Christ spoke of.

'In His will is our peace', says the Italian poet Dante Alighieri in his *Divine Comedy*.

Teaching and Preaching Adventist Core Beliefs in a Postmodern Context

Rolf J. Pöhler

Introduction

How we can effectively share Adventist beliefs with people who have a postmodern mindset? This is perhaps the greatest challenge the Church is facing currently in the secularised world. It makes me wonder: Are our theological seminaries and universities preparing future pastors and teachers adequately for their mission in the postmodern world? While our traditional, dogmatic teaching serves to confirm young believers in the faith and enables them to share it with interested people preferably with a Christian background, winning converts in a secular and postmodern culture requires a somewhat different approach. How can we adequately understand and convincingly present our fundamental beliefs in a culturally relevant and contextual way?

By way of introduction, I will first define the key terms used in the title of this essay.

Preaching and Teaching

In his Prolegomena of 1927, Karl Barth wrote: 'Die Aufgabe der Theologie ist eins mit der Aufgabe der Predigt.' This was his response to Adolf Harnack's assertion: 'Die Aufgabe der Theologie ist eins mit der Aufgabe der Wissenschaft.'[1] While we should not understand academic scholarship and evangelistic preaching as opposites (or even as adversaries), we should beyond that also be clear that our task as theologians is not limited to archaeological and historical research, exegetical and doctrinal analyses, theological and hermeneutical reflections, or pastoral and applied studies. In addition to all of that, it calls forth from us a desire to share these insights not only with our students in class but also with the people in the world today. If theology wants to avoid the charge of working in an ivory tower, theology teachers must also see themselves as preachers of the good news, effective communicators of the gospel to our own time and culture.

This is all the more important because we are also role models for our students who are preparing for pastoral ministry. Central to their task is the proclamation of 'the truth as it is in Jesus' (to quote a well-known phrase by Ellen White) and this implies the ability and desire to teach the Adventist message to the people attracted to Christ and his church (see Matt 28:19f.). If we want our students to become successful pastor-teachers (acc. to Eph 4:11ff.), we ourselves should strive to be teachers who are excited by the challenge of sharing God's truth with today's world. Thus, our theological seminaries and universities should be (or become) centres for secular and postmodern studies in their own right.

---

1   Karl Barth, *Die Lehre vom Worte Gottes: Prolegomena zur christlichen Dogmatik* (C. Kaiser, München, 1927), 6.

Adventist Core Beliefs

When I was a student at Andrews University in the 1970s, I became familiar with the six 'S-words', by which one can neatly summarise and easily memorise the distinctive teachings of Seventh-day Adventism: the Sabbath, the Sanctuary, the Second Advent, the State of the Dead, the Spirit of Prophecy, and the SDA Church. This list is reminiscent of a famous statement made in 1889 by Ellen White regarding the 'old landmarks' and what is included (and not included) in them[2]. Omitting from this list the so-called 'Spirit of Prophecy' (the focus of which is not doctrinal, but rather hermeneutical), we may come up with a simple cross-shaped figure that points in four different directions: ← Sabbath (past), → Second Advent (future), ↑ Sanctuary (above) and ↓ State of the Dead (below). Placing Christ and his atonement in the centre as 'the great truth around which all other truths cluster'[3], we may consider it for our present purpose as a useful definition of what we mean by 'Adventist core beliefs'.

Postmodern Culture

Much has been written about the cultural phenomenon that is being called 'postmodernism' and its various characteristics. Rather than repeating what others have already said or trying to add to their insights, I will simply mention what I consider to be the three most distinguishing and defining features of postmodern culture: individualism, relativism and pluralism. In distinction and marked contrast to the modern period preceding it (dating from the eighteenth to the twentieth centuries), contemporary postmodernism has lost confidence in the ability of human reason to discover objective truth valid for all times and people. Instead, it focuses on one's subjective experience by which we construct our own reality, choose our personal values and develop our individual faith. (In contrast to secular people, many postmoderns are open to religious experiences and are aware of their spiritual needs.) As a result, everyone may hold his or her own 'truths' without questioning the validity of other people's perspective,

---

2   Ellen G. White, *Counsels to Writers and Editors* (Nashville, TN: Southern Publishing Association, 1946), 30ff.
3   Ellen G. White, *Evangelism* (Washington, DC: Review and Herald Publishing Association, 1946), 190, see also 184-93.

world view, value system or religion. There are growing indications of Beliebigkeit (randomness) and of so-called 'patchwork religion'.

It needs no arguing that this situation poses an enormous challenge to the Seventh-day Adventist Church and its belief system. In the past (and in some regions of the world even today), Adventists could demonstrate with the help of Scripture and reason the soundness and even superiority of their doctrinal views over against the 'erroneous' teachings of other denominations, religions and philosophies. Today, many people could not care less for the doctrinal truths we hold so dear. To them, they seem largely irrelevant, devoid of real meaning, and quite unrelated to their personal lives and concerns. No matter how much we may decry the perceived and actual evils of individualism, relativism and pluralism, we need to find better and more effective ways of reaching our contemporaries with the 'truth' and attracting them to the Church, if we want to fulfil our common mission as Christians as well as our special commission as Seventh-day Adventists. This applies particularly in Europe, North America, and the South Pacific region.

I will now consider the presuppositions and conditions, hindrances and possibilities, forms and methods of sharing our basic Christian worldview in general as well as our Adventist beliefs and values in particular under the cultural conditions of the postmodern societies of today. This necessitates theological considerations, conceptual analyses as well as some practical applications.

Christian Apologetics and the Mission of the Church

Apologetics is the science of the rational and empirical explanation of the Christian and/or Adventist faith and theology to anyone in today's cultural context with the goal of reaching others convincingly on their own ground. Apologetics involves the encounter and interaction of the Christian and Adventist faith with the people and issues of our time in order to demonstrate its value with the aid of reason and experience.

This view of the nature and task of apologetics is based on the New Testament understanding of the mission of the church in the world. In 1 Peter 3:13-17, Christians are admonished to respond properly in word and deed to people who may question or even attack their faith in an unfriendly or aggressive manner. In this context, the apostle Peter formulates what may be called the 'Magna Carta' of Christian apologetics: 'Always be prepared to give an answer [ἀπολογίαν] to everyone who asks you to give the reason [λόγον] for the hope that you have. But do this with gentleness and respect.' (1 Pet 3:15 NIV/TNIV; cf. 1 Pet 2:12)

Thus, apologetics involves the justification and defence of the faith in response to critical questions and false accusations. Standing at the judgement bar of a critically minded and hostile society (at times, even in courtrooms), believers should, in a friendly manner, explain their hope and faith. The responsive, explanatory and witnessing character of their answer (ἀπολογίαν) conveys no negative implications whatsoever regarding their way of reasoning (λόγον) – quite contrary to the image attached to the term 'apologetics' today. In the biblical sense, apologetics has nothing to do with aggressiveness, defensiveness or dogmatism. In other words, we need loving apologists, not narrow-minded apologisers.

As the life and teachings of the apostle Paul admirably demonstrate, proper apologetics involves the conscious attempt to understand others and to be understood by others. When dealing with Jews, Paul reasoned from the Scriptures, using rabbinical forms of argumentation (Schriftbeweis) in order to convince them of Christ. In the presence of Gentiles such as in Athens, he resorted to a somewhat philosophical approach, intentionally building common ground (Argumentationsplattform) with the Stoic and Epicurean philosophers and also quoting Greek poets before giving his testimony regarding Christ and the resurrection (Acts 17:16ff.). His missionary strategy, outlined in 1 Cor 9:19-23, of establishing as many points of contact (Anknüpfungspunkte) as possible, by which he could come closer to others in order to bring them closer to Christ, is daring and challenging to the very core.

Becoming all things to all people in order to win some for Christ–this is nothing but the incarnational and relational approach of Jesus who identified himself fully with us in order to bring us back to God. To him, building bridges to the hearts and minds of people was more than an evangelistic method or even a missionary lifestyle; rather, it was his very nature. Seen from this perspective, it becomes clear what the apologetic task of the Church actually entails: firstly, listening to others with empathy in order to truly understand them, their questions and concerns; secondly, speaking in their cultural language and thought pattern so that they can fully understand what we are trying to communicate;

and, thirdly, sharing with them the eternal gospel as the plan and will of God for their life. Such a dialogical and contextual apologetics appears to be the only proper approach to Christian mission and Adventist evangelism, particularly in a postmodern setting. At its heart, it is all about communication. Thus, pastors and teachers of divine truth are first and foremost communicators.

The Adventist Church and the Postmodern Audience

This brings us to the following question: How secular and postmodern should Adventist preaching and teaching become? What are the limits beyond which the truth of God would be actually betrayed rather than faithfully transmitted? In an article entitled 'How "Secular" Should Adventist Theology Be?', Fritz Guy distinguished intentional secularism in the form of naturalistic humanism, agnosticism and atheism from practical secularism that considers God to be simply irrelevant today, constituting the greatest challenge to Adventism today. He summarised his answer in the following sentence: 'We should meet secularism on its own ground, talk its language, and relate the Adventist message to its concerns.... The Adventist message is to be translated into the language of secularism, but it must never be reduced to an echo.'[4]

What is true for secular people applies also to the postmodern audience. The Gospel must be preached afresh and told in new ways to every generation, since every generation has its own unique questions. Are we able and willing to meet our contemporaries on their own ground? Are we sensitive to their deeper, spiritual needs hidden behind the consuming lust for 'bread and games' as in ancient Rome? Church father Augustine knew from his own experience that the human heart is restless until it finds rest in God. Seen in this light, the Adventist message answers the deepest longing of humanity: While faith in the Creator-God provides meaning to our human existence, the Saviour offers freedom from guilt; on the Sabbath we may enjoy rest in a holistic way; the parousia of Christ gives hope for the future; and the church strives to be a loving and accepting community.

---

4   Fritz Guy, 'How "Secular" Should Adventist Theology Be?–Part 1' *Ministry*, October 1974, 9. See also 'How "Secular" Should Adventist Theology Be?–Part 2' *Ministry*, November 1974, 8-9.

In order to reach postmodern people with this life-saving message, it must be packaged in an appealing and non-threatening way. Instead of presenting doctrinal truths in a theoretical manner, they need to be shared in a way that is appealing to the whole person, including the emotions and everyday life. While biblical knowledge, human rationality and logical reasoning are not to be downgraded (cf. Acts 8:30f.), they need to be supplemented and strengthened by authentic personal experience (John 17:7), subjectivity and passion (Erlebnisorientierung). An open-minded and conversational approach does more to gain the attention of postmodern people than the presumption to know absolute truth. There needs to be room for personal insights and views as well as an acceptance of individual responsibility in matters of faith and life(style).

Paramount in this regard are the building and nurturing of genuine relationships, both to God (John 17:3; Matt 28:19) and among people. While postmoderns are suspicious of organised religion, they are open for a loving community in which they can grow spiritually and mature as whole persons. In short, the relational truths of the Christian and Adventist faith must be presented in a truly relational way. As noted above, mission is first and foremost about communication.

The Eternal Gospel as Truth for Today

Jerald Whitehouse, former director of the Global Centre for Adventist-Muslim Relations, has pointed out that the contextual communication of the gospel fosters diversity that is, at the same time, a prerequisite for the unity of the Church. From this he concludes: 'We must also allow and encourage each cultural group to discover the eternal truths for themselves and express their response to those truths in ways meaningful to them.'[5] In response to this challenge, the General Conference of Seventh-day Adventists through its Global Mission Issues Committee has set up several Research Centres dealing with the leading religions of the world: Islam, Buddhism, Hinduism, Judaism, Animism–and Postmodernism.

Commenting on this move to communicate Adventist beliefs to people in a non-Christian context, Jon Dybdahl, chair of the Department of Mission at

---

5   Jerald Whitehouse, 'That We Might Win Some', *Adventist Review*, 11 June 1998, 11.

Andrews University at the time, said: 'Our 27 [28] Fundamental Beliefs were written in relation to other Christians. Now we need to express them in the context of other religions.'[6] This raises an intriguing question: How would a postmodern version of the Fundamental Beliefs possibly read? In 2010, the Centre for Secular and Postmodern Studies published a book on Adventist beliefs specially geared towards postmodern readers. When the editor asked me to write the chapter on the three angels' messages, I accepted the challenge. After all, how could we as pastors and/or teachers dare to shy away from the task of effectively communicating the eternal gospel to the people of our time?! It is interesting to see how the sixteen contributors are using a new evangelistic paradigm.[7]

Some years ago, I had the opportunity to write two books presenting Adventist beliefs to a contemporary audience. While they are not specifically addressed to secular and/or postmodern readers, nevertheless they were planned and written with such people in mind. The first book is entitled *Christsein heute: Gelebter Glaube*[8] ('Vibrant Christianity: Living the Faith in Today's World') and is a kind of extended 'business card' of the Adventist Church in the German-speaking countries. In writing the manuscript I tried to implement what I had learned about addressing a postmodern audience by giving religious experience its due place over against abstract theological conceptions.

The second book *Hoffnung, die uns trägt: Wie Adventisten ihren Glauben bekennen*[9] ('Journey of Hope: An Adventist Confession of Faith') has been compared by a Protestant reviewer to an Evangelical catechism[10], because it presents the 28 Fundamental Beliefs in a readable contemporary style while, at the same time, aiming at doctrinal relevance and theological depth. In a concluding chapter, I have tried to express Adventist core beliefs in a nutshell centred

---

6   Adventist News Network (ANN) *Bulletin*, 9 April 2002.
7   *Experiencing the Joy: 42 Bible Talks*, eds. Miroslav Pujic and Sarah K. Asaftei (Stanborough Park, Garston, Watford, UK: Seventh-day Adventist Church in the British Isles, 2010). The contributors include: Radisa Antic, Reinder Bruinsma, Richard Daly, Daniel Duda, Jon Dybdahl, Jonathan Gallagher, Karen Holford, Don McFarlane, Holly Messenger, Rolf Pöhler, Miroslav Pujic, Gifford Rhamie, Cindy Tutsch, Laurence Turner, Bertil Wiklander, Richard Willis.
8   Rolf Pöhler, *Christsein heute: Gelebter Glaube* (Lüneburg: Advent-Verlag, 2007).
9   Rolf Pöhler, *Hoffnung, die uns trägt: Wie Adventisten ihren Glauben bekennen* (Lüneburg: Advent-Verlag, 2007).
10 Dr. theol. Walter Fleischmann-Bisten, email to info@adventisten.de July 4, 2008.

around the experiential themes of justice (second advent), freedom (Sabbath) and fellowship (church).

Together, these books form the nucleus of a multimedia concept of the German Publishing House and the two German Unions aimed at reaching out to the contemporary world. Personally I feel privileged to have had to face the challenge of expressing my personal faith in a way that is true to Adventist teachings, faithful to the Scriptures and appealing to contemporary readers. I wish that each one of us would be challenged in some similar manner. For it could help us all in the task of preaching and teaching Adventist core beliefs in a postmodern context.

Summary and Conclusion

In sum, I say 'Yes' to the importance of the individual believer, to the relative dimension of all human (including religious) knowledge, and to the plural aspects of the Christian and Adventist faith. But while I recognise individuality, relativity and diversity, I also say 'No' to the extreme notions of postmodern individualism, relativism and pluralism. What the Church and our culture need (and rarely achieve) is a healthy balance between the individual and the community, the relative and the absolute, unity and diversity. We may ignore this only at the peril of fostering polarising trends in church and society that will do more harm than good.

Selected Literature

Paulien, Jon, *Present Truth in the Real World: Faith in a Secular Society*, Boise, ID: PPPA, 1993.

Paulien, Jon, *Everlasting Gospel, Ever-changing World: Introducing Jesus to a Sceptical Generation*, Nampa, ID: PPPA, 2008.

Pöhler, Rolf J., *Christsein heute–Gelebter Glaube*, ed. Freikirche der STA. Lüneburg: Saatkorn-Verlag, Abt. Advent-Verlag, 2007.

Pöhler, Rolf J., *Hoffnung, die uns trägt: Wie Adventisten ihren Glauben bekennen*, ed. Freikirche der STA: Lüneburg: Saatkorn-Verlag, Abt. Advent-Verlag, 2008.

Pöhler, Rolf J., 'Religious Pluralism: A Challenge to the Contemporary Church' , in *Cast the Net on the Right Side ... Seventh-day Adventists Face the 'Isms'* , Newbold College, Bracknell, Berkshire, England: European Institute of World Mission, 1993, 81-89.

White, Ellen G., *Counsels to Writers and Editors*, Nashville, TN: Southern Publishing Association, 1946.

White, Ellen G., *Evangelism*, Washington, DC: Review and Herald Publishing Association, 1946.

Whitehouse, Jerald, 'That We Might Win Some' , *Adventist Review*, 11 June 1998, 8-11.

Part 3
Theological Perspectives

Our Place in God's Story:
Towards a Narrative Ecclesiology

Tihomir Lazic

This chapter seeks to interrogate and potentially enrich the prevailing ecclesiological paradigm that has shaped the discourse about the church since the late twentieth century. Its central hypothesis is that the underutilised narrative approach offers a promising methodology for furthering the understanding of the church as a divine-human community. This approach, I will argue, bypasses the usual constraints of the established communion ecclesiology methods, enabling a more nuanced, biblically grounded, and theologically comprehensive vision of believers' shared life in God.

Given that contemporary ecclesiologists have not yet fully traversed this path, it becomes essential to illuminate the theological underpinnings of this approach and offer initial explanations of how it might work. While a full systematic articulation of this relational vision of the church exceeds the scope of this chapter, I do hope to lay the groundwork for such a task by offering preliminary methodological considerations. Accordingly, to chart a narrative course within contemporary ecclesiology, some initial adjudications need to be made about the following key components: the choice of the overarching methodological pathway, modes of reasoning, discursive tools, epistemic horizon, and critically, the underpinning role of biblical theology in this cross-disciplinary quest for a holistic ecclesial vision. The primary focus will be on the central ecclesiastical element: the relationship between the triune God and the church.

Through this reflection, I hope to lay down basic methodological and constructive guidelines for rooting our vision of the church in the life of God.

Church in the Making

An unprecedented resurgence of interest in ecclesiology has marked the theological landscape of the last half century.[1] This ecclesiological renaissance can be attributed, in part, to the rise of the ecumenical movement, which underscores the necessity of a preliminary understanding of the church's essence to discuss its unity. The underlying logic is that one cannot unify entities without comprehending the organisms one aims to amalgamate. This perspective has further led to the appearance of fresh concepts and language designed to bridge the existing ecclesiological divides and to coalesce on articulating the church's essence.[2]

Following Vatican II, the term *koinonia*–commonly translated as *communio* in Latin, or 'communion' or 'fellowship' in English–arose as a pivotal concept in the contemporary characterisation of the Christian church.[3] By attempting to integrate its rival theological proposals, *koinonia* swiftly earned international acclaim as one of the most invigorating and promising constructs in the contemporary ecclesial dialogue. Over time, it became almost impossible to write or talk about the relational core of the church without employing this term. Due to the popularity of its foundational concept, communion ecclesiology is now hailed

---

[1] Gerard Manon and Lewis Symour Mudge, *The Routledge Companion to the Christian Church* (New York; London: Routledge, 2008), 1. Given its preoccupation with ecclesiological concerns, the twentieth century is often called the 'century of ecclesiology'. See, Otto Dibelius, *Das Jahrhundert Der Kirche: Geschichte, Betrachtung, Umschau und Ziele* (Berlin: Furche-Verlag, 1927). A famous Lutheran theologian, Jaroslav Pelikan, described this ecclesiological renaissance of the twentieth-century in the following way: 'The doctrine of the Church became, as it had never quite been before, the bearer of the whole of the Christian message for the twentieth century, as well as the recapitulation of the entire doctrinal tradition from preceding centuries.' See, Jaroslav Pelikan, *Christian Doctrine and Modern Culture (since 1700)* (Chicago: University of Chicago Press, 1989), 282.

[2] Veli-Matti Kärkkäinen, *Introduction to Ecclesiology: Ecumenical, Historical & Global Perspectives* (Downers Grove, IL: InterVarsity Press, 2002), 7-11.

[3] Lorelei F. Fuchs, *Koinonia and the Quest for an Ecumenical Ecclesiology: From Foundations through Dialogue to Symbolic Competence for Communionality* (Grand Rapids, MI: Eerdmans, 2008), 25-43; Herwi Rikhof, *The Concept of Church: A Methodological Inquiry into the Use of Metaphors in Ecclesiology* (London: Sheed and Ward, 1981) 233-35.

by many as the essential and most fundamental form of ecclesiology. Today, it is universally acknowledged among ecclesiologists that the church represents the communion of believers, both with one another and with the triune God.[4]

At its core, communion ecclesiology is a specific type of ecclesiology that describes the church in terms of relationships.[5] The primary aim of this kind of ecclesiology is to give a clear articulation to the dynamic interplay that exists between the persons of the Trinity (trinitarian communion), human beings and the triune God (vertical communion), the members of the communion of the faithful (horizontal communion), the local and universal church, and the church and the non-church. This relational ecclesiological discourse defines the church as a communion of persons united with God in Christ through the Holy Spirit.[6]

Evidently, communion ecclesiology's principal aspiration is to ground the community of believers in the life of the triune God. Most communion authors writing in the last half-century agree that how we perceive God's role in forming the community significantly shapes the basic orientation and structures of believers' shared life.[7] They have therefore attempted to add breadth and depth to the sociological definitions of the term 'community' (*koinonia*) by exploring the ways in which the human community reflects and participates in the trinitarian communion.

These two major approaches–*imitatio Trinitatis* and *participatio Trinitatis*– are currently at the forefront of the contemporary ecclesiological conversation when it comes to clarifying the relationship between the Trinity and the church. In order to determine which one of these two, if either, is a more promising methodological route for articulating a dynamic and biblically rooted relational

---

4 World Council of Churches, *The Church: Towards a Common Vision, Faith and Order*. Paper No. 214 (Geneva: World Council of Churches Publications, 2013). See also: World Council of Churches, 'Towards Koinonia in Faith, Life, and Witness: A Discussion Paper', *Proceedings of the Fifth World Conference on Faith and Order in Santiago de Compostela* (Geneva: World Council of Churches Publications, 1993).
5 Dennis M. Doyle, *Communion Ecclesiology: Vision and Versions* (Maryknoll, NY: Orbis Books, 2000), 12; Fuchs, 25-43.
6 Tihomir Lazic, *Towards an Adventist Version of Communio Ecclesiology: Remnant in Koinonia, Pathways for Ecumenical and Interreligious Dialogue*, ed. by Gerard Mannion and Mark Chapman (Basingstoke: Palgrave Macmillan, 2019), 146-53.
7 Terry L. Cross, *The People of God's Presence: An Introduction to Ecclesiology* (Grand Rapids, MI: Baker Academic, 2019), 43.

vision of the church, it is necessary to consider briefly their main proposals, prospects, and limitations.[8]

The *Imitatio Trinitatis* Approach

The *imitatio Trinitatis* approach focuses on the church as an image of the triune God, positing that ecclesial relations mirror intra-trinitarian relations.[9] Hence, the inner-trinitarian *koinonia*, according to communion ecclesiologists, should be used as a structural blueprint for the human *koinonia*. Accepted as almost a standardised ecclesiological procedure, this approach ('from above') has been developed and applied extensively by a considerable number of mainline Christian theologians.[10]

The limitation of such an approach lies in its presumption of highly specific, reliable, and detailed knowledge of God's inner being and operations—a level of knowledge we as humans simply do not hold. It further creates an overly close parallel between the Creator and the created order, an ontological assumption that cannot be fully substantiated. This results in a speculative exercise, where human notions of community, derived from our interpersonal experiences,

---

[8] For a more detailed critical assessment of these dominant approaches, refer to my recent publication: Tihomir Lazic, 'Ecclesia Semper Migranda: Towards a Vision of a Migrant Church for Migrants', in *The Church, Migration, and Global (In)Difference?* (New York, NY: Palgrave Macmillan, 2021), 241-61.

[9] Scott MacDougall, *More Than Communion: Imagining an Eschatological Ecclesiology* (London: Bloomsbury T & T Clark, 2015), 76. For instance, Zizioulas defines the church as 'a set of relationships making up a mode of being, exactly as is the case of the Trinitarian God'. John D. Zizioulas, 'The Doctrine of the Holy Trinity: The Significance of the Cappadocian Contribution', in *Trinitarian Theology Today: Essays on Divine Being and Act*, ed. by Christoph Schwobel (Edinburgh: T. & T. Clark, 1995), 27.

[10] Within Catholic, Orthodox, and Protestant theological circles, the most coherent, creative, and profound theological attempts to define a vision of the church according to the image of a triune God have been made by Metropolitan John D. Zizioulas (Eastern-Orthodox tradition), Cardinal Joseph Ratzinger (who later became Pope Benedict XVI), and Miroslav Volf (Protestant/Evangelical and 'Free Church' tradition). See: John D. Zizioulas, *Being as Communion: Studies in Personhood and the Church* (Crestwood, NY: St. Vladimir's Seminary Press, 1985); Joseph Ratzinger, *Called to Communion: Understanding the Church Today* (San Francisco: Ignatius Press, 1996); Miroslav Volf, *After Our Likeness: The Church as the Image of the Trinity* (Grand Rapids, MI: William B. Eerdmans, 1998).

are projected onto our understanding of the dynamics of the trinitarian communion. In a sense, it appears to be recreating God in our image rather than the inverse.

The *imitatio Trinitatis* approach suffers from additional shortcomings. Notably, its proponents often overlook the sinful conditions of humanity due to their intense focus on applying a perfect trinitarian model to human relations, thereby neglecting human agency in church formation. This leads to idealised, static, ahistorical, and overly romanticised depictions of the church, detached from the messy realities of everyday life.[11]

Considering this assessment, I argue that the *imitatio Trinitatis* approach, despite its prevalent use in communion ecclesiology, may not be the optimal foundation for envisioning the church's integral role within God's life. Hence, we pivot to explore a less prominent, yet potentially more fruitful, methodological pathway within communion ecclesiology.

The *Participatio Trinitatis* Approach

The alternative methodological route, termed *participatio Trinitatis*, considers the relationship between the Trinity and the church in terms of the believer's active participation in the divine life as manifested in history. It underscores the dynamic personal interaction, indwelling, and mutual sharing, both among the believers and with God. Instead of speculating about the inner mode of being of the immanent Trinity, the *participatio Trinitatis* approach emphasises God's actions in the world (*opera Trinitatis ad extra*).[12] It bases the church's existence on those elements of divine life revealed and made accessible through the

---

11 For a more detailed assessment of the inadequacies of this approach, see: Tihomir Lazic, 'Church as Koinonia: Exploring the ecumenical potential of John Zizioulas's communio ecclesiology', in *Stolen Churches or Bridges to Orthodoxy?* Volume 1: Historical and Theological Perspectives on the Orthodox and Eastern Catholic Dialogue (New York, NY: Palgrave Macmillan, 2021), 317-37.

12 Paul S. Fiddes, *Participating in God: A Pastoral Doctrine of the Trinity* (Louisville, KY: Westminster John Knox Press, 2001).

tangible, reconciliatory event of Christ, wherein humans participate through the workings of the Spirit.[13]

Accordingly, I propose that this approach is at its best when it starts with a rich account of the movement of the Spirit among believers and then explores the ways in which the Spirit transforms and gathers believers around Christ, making them an essential part of God's story.[14] Hence, to attain a deeper understanding of the community-forming work carried out by Christ through the Spirit, it is crucial to give both pneumatology and Christology equal consideration in our construction of ecclesiology. This approach–recently gaining traction among theologians across Christian denominations–presents significant potential for fresh theological discoveries.[15] This is so, especially in view of the fact that it allows the Scripture to be used as the source and orienting framework for identifying and interpreting the community-generative movements of the Father, Son, and Holy Spirit as experienced in various historical and geographical settings.

With this in view, I suggest that the *participatio Trinitatis* approach offers a more robust methodological pathway than the *imitatio Trinitatis* approach. It is better suited for constructing a dynamic, nuanced, and biblically informed vision of a church's ever-deepening communion with God.[16]

---

13   For a more extensive exposition and assessment of this approach, see: Lazic, *Towards an Adventist Version of Communio Ecclesiology*, 183-90.
14   Gregory J. Liston, *The Anointed Church: Toward a Third Article Ecclesiology* (Minneapolis: Fortress Press, 2015), 12-14; Karl Barth, *The Humanity of God* (Richmond, VA: John Knox, 1972), 24-25; D. Lyle Dabney, 'Starting with the Spirit: Why the Last Should Now Be First', in *Starting with the Spirit*, ed. by Stephen K. Pickard and Gordon R. Preece (Hindmarsh, Adelaide, South Australia: Australian Theological Forum, 2001).
15   These include authors writing from the perspective of Roman Catholicism (Yves Congar, Ralph Del Colle, David Coffey), Protestant denominations (Lyle Dabney, Myk Habets, Gary Badcock, Clark Pinnock) and ecumenical traditions (Veli-Matti Kärkkäinen, Amos Yong, Miroslav Volf, Steven Studebaker). Liston, 14.
16   Yet, similarly to imitatio Trinitatis, this participatory framework is not immune to various forms of ecclesial reductionism. For that reason, certain well-established ecclesiological principles that have survived the test of time should be respected in the process of construction. To make sure that the trinitarian foundation of this participatory ecclesial framework is articulated adequately, I would like to propose that the following four regulative principles need to be respected in the process of ecclesiological construction: (1) the principle of indivisibility, (2) the principle of balance, (3) the principle of comprehensiveness, and (4) the principle of ontological embeddedness. These four principles

Essential Tools for Ecclesiological Construction

Now that we have identified the most suitable methodological pathway for probing the diverse aspects of believers' communal participation in the divine life, an ensuing question naturally arises: What mode of reasoning best encapsulates the intricacies of this dynamic relational interplay between God and humanity, on both individual and collective levels? Or more specifically, what heuristic categories and discursive tools could be most effective and pertinent in expressing the mystery embodied by the church? The response to these inquiries is crucial as it can reveal the essential components required for constructing ecclesiology.

In the annals of Christian history, myriad elucidatory strategies and tools have been implemented, each striving to grapple with and achieve a deeper comprehension and articulation of the multifaceted nature of the church.[17] Some traditions have chosen an indirect apophatic approach, articulating the essence of the church by negation, stating what it is not, a method known as *via negativa*, or adhering to a reverent silence regarding this or any other theological mystery. Conversely, other traditions have espoused a cataphatic perspective, deferring any resort to negation until the full potential of positive descriptions is exhausted. Among the affirmative strategies employed to elucidate the mystery of human communion with God, the use of analogies drawn from familiar experiences has been prevalent. This analogical path harnesses relatable devices such as metaphors, allegories, images, similes, types, and symbols.

For instance, when the authors of the New Testament sought to shed light on the nature of the church, their language was heavily reliant on imagery and metaphor. A notable work by Paul S. Minear identified as many as ninety-six distinct metaphors of the church within the New Testament.[18] Among the most

---

are intended to serve as basic guidelines, or correctives, in our attempt to develop a well-rounded and fully trinitarian vision of the ecclesial koinonia. These regulative principles safeguard the integrity of the believers' witness about who God is and how he is involved in originating, maintaining, and completing the life of the church. In so doing, they shed light on the nature, form, and extent of believers' personal and communal participation in the mysteries of divine life. For further explanation of these four principles, see: Lazic, *Towards an Adventist Version of Communio Ecclesiology*, 231-3.

17 Matt Jenson and David E. Wilhite, *The Church: A Guide for the Perplexed* (London: T. & T. Clark, 2010).
18 Paul Sevier Minear, *Images of the Church in the New Testament* (Cambridge: Clarke, 2007).

influential of these are the portrayals of the church as the people of God, the body of Christ, a fellowship of faith, the temple of the Spirit, the new creation, and others.[19] These New Testament metaphors are deeply rooted in the tangible, experiential spheres of life that the early Christians were immersed in, including corporeal, architectural, agricultural, martial, familial, marital, and other dimensions of existence.[20] Such cognitive devices, layered with profound evocative and heuristic potential, stimulate strong emotional resonance and loyalty, invoking the fullness of human participation, and thus enabling transformation.

A common thread that runs through this metaphor-rich approach, along with other analogous descriptions, is that they are intended to unveil what the church is by describing what the church is like. However, without contextual framing and further qualifications, these metaphoric descriptions may remain elusive and obscure. Even in the early Christian era, these metaphors were not immune from eclecticism, arbitrary interpretation, and subjectivity. This reality prompts a multitude of questions, including those concerning the criteria for metaphor selection and the theological and contextual parameters within which these images are to be interpreted and applied.

To lend further precision and reconcile some of these innate dilemmas, Christians have invoked a range of descriptors and defining attributes, collectively known as the marks of the church (*notae ecclesiae*). These marks serve as key identifiers of the church's nature and mission, aspiring to distil the essential features encapsulated by metaphors and analogies into more concrete terms, thereby aiding the church in its pursuit of a discernible identity.[21] They illuminate the church's ultimate *telos* and provide navigation, correction, guidelines, and benchmarks for a community of believers *in via*. Yet, despite their invaluable contribution, these ecclesial markers, much like the metaphors from which they are derived, face challenges when used in isolation–namely, undefined selection

---

19 John K. McVay, "Biblical Metaphors for the Church: Building Blocks for Ecclesiology," in *Message, Mission and the Unity of the Church: Studies in Adventist Ecclesiology*, vol. 2, ed. by Ángel Manuel Rodríguez (Silver Spring, MD: Biblical Research Institute, 2013); Reinder Bruinsma, *The Body of Christ: Biblical Understanding of the Church* (Hagerstown, MD: Review and Herald Publishing Association, 2009), 46-58.

20 John K. McVay, "Biblical Metaphors for the Church and Adventist Ecclesiology," in *Andrews University Seminary Studies* 44, no. 2 (2006): 285-315.

21 Jenson and Wilhite, *The Church*, 58-101.

criteria, interpretive ambiguity, and an inability to provide a holistic depiction of the church.

In response to these latent complexities, models have been devised as refined extensions of root metaphors. They provide an additional layer of analytical and synthetic processing, forming theoretical frameworks on the level of systematic, categorical thought. Models serve as intellectual constructs that proficiently explore and explain the multifaceted phenomena observed in the church. As highlighted by Avery Dulles, this approach is at its best when we juggle multiple models simultaneously, thereby adhering to the principle of complementarity for a more holistic understanding of the church.[22]

However, as with images and marks, employing a model-based approach necessitates a deliberate effort to address broader and more fundamental methodological questions pertaining to the presuppositional framework within which these models can effectively operate. A comprehensive interpretation of metaphors, marks, and models demands a conscientious evaluation not merely of their historical, sociological, and literary contexts of origin–contexts that govern their rightful interpretation, use, harmonisation, or further development. We must also illuminate the overarching theological context that dictates their application when articulating the life of the Spirit-engendered, Christ-centric community at various junctures of its historical journey with God. Only through such a holistic lens can we truly appreciate and capitalise on the full potential of these heuristic instruments of ecclesiological construction.

Why is it crucial to elucidate the overarching theistic worldview within which these analytical tools operate? The answer is compelling: in the absence of a clear delineation of this theological scaffold, these tools risk misappropriation and manipulation by external, reductionist narratives that permeate our society, as well as the prevalent cultural outlooks often adopted without question. The church's history provides a sobering reminder of the enduring allure of moulding our self-perception through the lens of secular culture.

While integration with secular culture is not innately detrimental–after all, the church needs to communicate, serve, and exist in a way that resonates with humanity's evolving needs, experiences, and modes of reasoning–it becomes a concern when biblical imagery is reshaped to conform more snugly with the

---

22   Avery Dulles, *Models of the Church* (New York: Image Books, 2002), 2.

church's existing operational realities. This can inadvertently sanction flawed relational patterns, threatening the church's mission and distorting believers' spiritual engagement. In such instances, the church unwittingly becomes a mouthpiece for the cultural narrative. The church's adoption of these images often occurs beneath the surface of awareness. However, their influence on shaping the church's life remains potent, possibly even amplified when unnoticed. Thus, it is critical to examine biblical analogies in their authentic contexts, illuminate hidden imagery, critically appraise our prevailing interpretations, and discover new descriptive figures that faithfully echo the biblical witness and resonate with us today.

Ponder on the innumerable portrayals of the church, potentially reflecting the impressions of Christendom, the Enlightenment, and consumerism. The church is likened to a shopping centre, a community hub, a corporation, a theatre, a classroom, a hospital, a spa, a motivational seminar, campaign headquarters, a social advocacy group, and more. These images might reflect the manifold activities that are an essential and legitimate part of the Christian calling, such as teaching, aiding the underprivileged, and forging social connections. However, issues emerge when we forget the foundational biblical narrative and the church's inherent character within it, and these activities, stripped of their authentic ecclesial spirit, are informed by an alien narrative.[23]

Therefore, we must confront these essential questions: Which narrative is sculpting our self-perception? What underlying story governs our use of images, marks, and models in articulating our communal identity? The church can only rectify the distortion brought about by alien narratives and images by returning to its roots–the biblical narrative and its symbiotic images.[24] Sometimes, to move forward, we must go back to the beginning.

---

23 Michael W. Goheen, *Light to the Nations: The Missional Church and the Biblical Story* (Grand Rapids, MI: Baker Academy, 2011), 15-17.

24 To truly honour the Bible's normative role (*sola scriptura*), place it above yet in harmony with other sources of divine revelation (*prima scriptura*), and explore the entirety of prophetic and apostolic testimonies within both the Old and New Testaments (*tota scriptura*), we must acknowledge the divine-human origins of Scripture, and thereby its epistemic authority for Christians' faith and life. It is a guiding light for the use of metaphors, marks, models, and other forms of expression in constructing a comprehensive ecclesial vision.

The Foundational Role of Biblical Theology

As we continue our discussion, we need to acknowledge the foundational role that biblical theology plays in the architecture of ecclesiology. This discipline delves deep into the worldview(s) of biblical authors, casting light on the foundational theological narrative that provides lucidity and context to the linguistic devices used to describe the church. Understanding the church's role within this unfolding divine narrative and the original intent of these ecclesial descriptors demands a holistic study. Such study should extend beyond the mere dissection of isolated texts within their most immediate contexts and should avoid hasty extrapolation to contemporary applications or the formulation of overly neat theoretical systems. Here, biblical theology carves out its indispensable role in the complex matrix of human inquiry into the truth of divine revelation, bridging the gap between disciplines such as biblical studies, pastoral studies, and historical/systematic theology.

I contend that this discipline truly excels when it acknowledges the ultimate revelation of God in Jesus Christ–the embodied Word–while also affirming that God, in his boundless wisdom and grace, has orchestrated the inscription and the collection of a canon of divinely inspired writings. These comprise both antecedent and subsequent human testimonies about Christ–reliable, yet imperfect. Here, Scripture, the written Word of God, is viewed not only as a record and a product but also as a vital instrument in God's mission of reconciliation.[25] Breathed and moulded by the Spirit, Scripture guides humanity towards a deeper communion with God.

This unflinchingly theistic and dynamic approach to the origins and nature of Scripture–a stance that may not be widely favoured among contemporary scholars of Scripture–profoundly appreciates both its divine and human aspects.[26] It unveils a rich tapestry of intricate connections and harmonies within

---

25   Christopher J. H. Wright, *The Great Story and the Great Commission: Participating in the Biblical Drama of Mission* (Grand Rapids, MI: Baker Academic, 2023), 1-11.
26   This view broadly resembles 'the dynamic theory' of Biblical inspiration as found in Millard J. Erickson, *Introducing Christian Doctrine* (Grand Rapids, MI: Baker Academic, 2015), 52-53. Similarly, see Fernando L. Canale, *The Cognitive Principle of Christian Theology: A Hermeneutical Study of the Revelation and Inspiration of the Bible* (Berrien Springs, MI: Andrews University Lithotech, 2005); *Biblical Hermeneutics: An Adventist Approach*, ed. by

the biblical text, deftly steering clear of potentially distortive reductionisms. On one side, it eludes docetic inclinations that overly accentuate the divine at the cost of eclipsing the fragile, culturally conditioned human voice. On the other, it shuns ebionitic tendencies that overemphasise the human agency while failing to discern the subtle touch of divine inspiration and providence. This divine guidance has preserved the distinct voices of human witnesses without causing distortion, excessive separation, fusion, or suppression.[27]

In this manner, the approach recognises the polyphony of human testimony, each voice distinct yet intertwined in a divine symphony, which tells the cosmic story of God. It promotes a harmonious coexistence of the divine and the human, celebrating each distinctive voice as it contributes to the grand narrative without succumbing to forced unification or divisive fragmentation. From this standpoint on the nature, epistemic status, and interpretation of Scripture, it becomes pertinent to ask: What is the epistemic horizon within which the Bible-shaped, theologically robust, and contextually attuned vision of the church takes root and thrives?

Towards a Theodramatic Horizon

In our quest to uncover the most fitting epistemic horizon that allows a rich expression of the ecclesiological vision to surface, we will proceed with a two-pronged investigation involving both systematic and biblical theology. By intertwining these disciplines, we hope to bridge any perceived gaps and foster a more holistic ecclesiological understanding.

From a systematic theology perspective, it is important to acknowledge Nicholas Healy's influential book *Church, World and the Christian Life: Practical-Prophetic Ecclesiology*, which has played a significant role in reshaping and broadening ecclesiology over the past two decades.[28] Healy draws on a critical

---

Frank M. Hasel (Silver Spring, MD: Biblical Research Institute, 2021); John C. Peckham, *Canonical Theology: The Biblical Canon, Sola Scriptura, and Theological Method* (Grand Rapids: Eerdmans, 2016).

27 Though rooted in patristic Christological debates, referencing Ebionism and Docetism, these terms have evolved to illuminate the divine-human dynamic in broader theological discussions.

28 Nicholas M. Healy, *Church, World, and the Christian Life: Practical- Prophetic Ecclesiology*, Cambridge Studies in Christian Doctrine (Cambridge, UK; New York: Cambridge University Press, 2000).

aspect of Hans Urs van Balthasar's theology, his theodramatic theory, to address some of the inherent limitations of traditional 'blueprint' ecclesiologies.[29] Van Balthasar insists that theological discourse should emulate the true character of revelation and Christian existence before the eschaton. He envisions the relationships between God, the world, and the church as a play. Two primary Christian horizons and theological styles are presented in this context: the epic and the dramatic.

Epic theology assumes an external observer's stance, stepping outside the immediate drama to contemplate the entire play in its completed form. This perspective is often visible in church documents, catechisms, and large-scale systematic theologies, which present the Christian life as a finished, neatly organised whole. By distancing itself from the fray, epic theology cultivates a streamlined account of Christian doctrine, often operating under the assumption that the shared life of the church adheres to a preordained, mechanistic script. While this static and ahistorical approach can offer some valuable panoramic insights, its dominance can potentially be detrimental. It risks overlooking emergent themes in the unfolding drama, and by diminishing or simplifying inherent tensions of Christian existence, it could yield rigid and overly tidy essentialist portrayals that skew the complex realities of the faith experience.

Contrastingly, dramatic theology adopts the vantage point of an active participant immersed in the ongoing play of existence. It emphasises the tensions and conflicts inherent in Christian life, mirroring in its form the continuous, dynamic struggle that underpins discipleship. Thus, this perspective affirms the experiential, relational, embodied, and evolving character of the faith journey. Healy rightfully argues that a theodramatic or metanarrative horizon is particularly suited for reshaping ecclesiology as a practical-prophetic discipline, skilfully holding in balance the delicate tension between divine and human aspects which might otherwise blur, detach or tilt towards a single side. This dynamic horizon enables a nuanced, layered portrayal of the church that acknowledges

---

29 Hans Urs von Balthasar, *Theo-Drama: Theological Dramatic Theory* (San Francisco, CA: Ignatius Press, 1988). The metaphor of drama is also used in Robert W. Jenson, *Systematic Theology: The Triune God* (New York: Oxford University Press, 1997), 75.

both its divine orientation and origins and its human limitations, all while situating it within the ongoing drama of human-divine historical interaction.

According to Healy's assessment, the epic horizon underpins most of the modern 'blueprint' ecclesiological accounts, implying a final, propositional, normative, timeless, and all-encompassing account of church doctrine, potentially insufficient for any future context or development. As evidenced in our previous discussion regarding the *imitatio Trinitatis* approach to communion ecclesiology, these representations often neglect the flawed, messy, practical, sinful, and historical reality of human participation in God within ever-changing, real-life contexts. To avoid these constraints and allow a more dynamic ecclesial vision to emerge, he proposes a shift away from a rigid church definition to a focus on the dramatic patterns traced throughout church history. This theodramatic approach sees theological inquiry as an evolving, open-ended process, not constrained by a single model or secular narrative but informed by the scriptural narrative of creation and redemption.[30]

At this juncture, the dialogue within systematic theology intersects with recent methodological advancements within biblical theology. An increasing number of biblical theology scholars are advocating an implementation of a narrative or theodramatic approach,[31] proposing it as the most fruitful and promising lens for comprehending the entirety of biblical witness in its canonical structure.[32] Employing this narrative lens provides a rich backdrop for meaningfully exploring the evolution of the church's identity amidst shifting historical circumstances and challenges. In turn, it facilitates the holistic incorporation of the church's identity, discipleship, and mission into an overarching story of God unveiled in Scripture. Building upon this perspective, Gunnar Pedersen's significant contributions to biblical theology deserve consideration, and

---

30   Healy, 25-76.
31   Though the terms 'story' and 'drama' may hold distinct connotations, for the purposes of this discussion, we will use them interchangeably with the understanding that we are referring to a dynamic, ongoing narrative movement that invites and involves active participation.
32   Craig Bartholomew, *Introducing Biblical Hermeneutics: A Comprehensive Framework for Hearing God in Scripture* (Grand Rapids: Baker Academic, 2015).

his methodological proposals could provide valuable groundwork for future advancements in narrative ecclesiology.

Our Story in God's Story

Gunnar Pedersen has dedicated his scholarly pursuits to formulating a compelling argument for a theological hermeneutics approach that embraces the theistic and narrative attributes of the biblical text. His seminal development, termed the 'theistic-narrative method of biblical theology', positions the Bible as an expansive meta-narrative–wherein lies a wealth of literary genres and devices–awaiting exploration and comprehension. In concert with distinguished scholars, including James Barr, Brevard Childs, James Sanders, Walter C. Kaiser, N. T. Wright, Craig G. Bartholomew, Desmond T. Alexander, Michael W. Goheen, among others, Pedersen subscribes to the assertion of our residence within a 'storied' universe. He also upholds that this universe's essence is truthfully captured by biblical writers in narrative form. In essence, he contends that the Bible presents a story–a grand narrative with a beginning, middle, and end. This story unfolds from creation, leads to a new creation, and in between, narrates the complex relationship between humanity and God, marked by sin and salvation.

Accordingly, Pedersen maintains that biblical theology's supreme task is to delve into the story inhabited by its authors–a story through which they perceive the world and derive meaning for their discourse. He asserts that these biblical authors, as direct participants in this grand narrative, do not simply chronicle historical events. Instead, they interpret the 'inside' meaning of these events, weaving them into the fabric of this overarching story. Discerning the meanings and the internal dynamics of this narrative–with its rich tapestry of characters, plotlines, key themes, tensions, and stages–is indispensable for those who aspire to understand the underlying worldview and epistemic horizon of these biblical authors.[33]

The narrative these authors inhabit and engage with profoundly shapes their perspectives, values, and identities, providing a sense of unity, purpose, and

---

33   Gunnar Pedersen, "The Bible as "Story": A Methodological Opportunity', in *Exploring the Frontiers of Faith: Festschrift in Honour of Dr. Jan Paulsen*, ed. by Børge Schantz and Reinder Bruinsma (Lueneburg, Germany: Advent-Verlag,

continuity across time. It helps them to imprint significance onto select historical events and developments, underlining their formative influence on the trajectory of the grand cosmic story. Thus, the central responsibility of biblical theology is to unearth this story-shaped worldview, enabling the Bible to tell its story/stories on its own terms, not those of its readers (notwithstanding their importance in their respective contexts), be they from the past or present.

Gunnar Pedersen and Jan Barna have embarked on an insightful scholarly partnership, co-authoring several pivotal academic works that have had a significant impact on their Adventist colleagues and many of their theology students.[34] Together, they assert that this story, with its onward momentum, moves from an auspicious beginning through a looming conflict, engaging in a lengthy process characterised by promises and fulfilments–all geared towards resolving the conflict and ultimately leading to a hopeful ending. This dramatic movement progresses in seven major acts (stages), with a huge cast of actors (including us), all playing their part in an expansive narrative whose Author and Director is God himself. These seven successive stages include (1) Creation, (2) the Fall, (3) the Promise and the People (Israel), (4) the Fulfilment in Jesus, (5) the Fulfilment and the People (Church), (6) the Day of the Lord (consisting of the three phases of the universal judgement), and (7) the New Creation. Each of these stages is discernible because of major transitional events or divine salvific actions, which advance the cosmic story of restoration from Creation to New Creation.[35]

This theistic-narrative framework has important ecclesiological implications. As Christopher J. H. Wright aptly observed, 'the Bible clearly reveals God who drives the whole story of the universe forward with a sense of divine purpose and ultimate destiny, who also calls into existence a people who share in that divine mission, a people with an identity and role within the plan of God.'[36] This means that for constructing a biblically rooted ecclesiological vision of believers' communal participation in God, it is necessary to know the overarching narrative

---

2009), 237-45.

34 Gunnar Pedersen and Jan Barna, 'Towards a Biblical Theology Method: A 7-stage Theistic-Narrative Methodology', unpublished paper presented at Tyndale Fellowship, Cambridge, UK, 7-9 July 2011; Gunnar Pedersen and Jan Barna, 'A Search for the Biblical Epistemic Horizon: Towards Meta-Hermeneutics', *Spes Christiana*, 32.2. 2021, 23-44.

35 For a brief description of these stages, see: Jan Barna, 'The Grand Story', *Ministry*, March 2012, 20-22, 24.

36 Wright, *The Great Story and the Great Commission*, xi.

they are a part of, as well as their current location within this unfolding story.[37] With the aid of this guiding narrative structure, one can begin to articulate what the community of Christ's followers is supposed to be and do in response to what Christ is doing at any given stage of the ongoing cosmic story of redemption.

Central to this perspective is the acknowledgement that God's cosmic restoration plan incorporates a particular group of people. Both 'particular' and 'people' carry weight here. God elects a people to contribute to his universal purpose. This election denotes a historical particularity–a people at a specific time and place. The biblical narrative moves from the universal to the particular before ultimately expanding back to the universal, a final shift that transpires both historically and geographically. Historically, the biblical account progresses via a specific conduit to reach a universal end, moving from a single nation to encompass all nations. Geographically, the narrative flow extends from one location to all locations, from Jerusalem (or further back, from Eden) to the earth's furthest reaches.[38] This focus on particularity shapes most of the biblical story. However, as Richard Bauckham astutely notes, 'this particularised focus stands between two universal bookends: creation and consummation. The story begins with God's creation of the entire earth and the progenitors of all peoples. The story ends with the new creation and a people from all nations.'[39] This further entails that the community of believers is to fulfil its divine purpose precisely within this flow of God's cosmic restoration that broadens from the particular to the universal.

N. T. Wright explains the instrumental role of the Scripture in mobilising and integrating God's people–both individually and communally–within the cosmic story of God. He suggests that the Bible should be read and understood:

---

37 Craig G. Bartholomew and Michael W. Goheen, *The Drama of Scripture: Finding Our Place in the Biblical Story*, 2nd ed. (Grand Rapids, MI: Baker Academic, 2014).
38 Michael W. Goheen and Christopher J. H. Wright, "Mission and Theological Interpretation," in *A Manifesto for Theological Interpretation*, ed. by Craig G. Bartholomew and Heath A. Thomas (Grand Rapids, MI: Baker Academic, 2016), 175-6.
39 Richard Bauckham, *Bible and Mission: Christian Witness in a Postmodern World* (Grand Rapids, MI: Baker Academic, 2003), 13-16; and Richard Bauckham, "Mission as Hermeneutics for Scriptural Interpretation," in Goheen, *Reading the Bible Missionally*, 28-44.

> [...] as yet unfinished drama, which contained its own impetus, its own forward movement, which demanded to be concluded in the proper manner but which required of the actors a responsible entering into the story as it stood, in order first to understand how the threads could appropriately be drawn together, and then to put that understanding into effect by speaking and acting with both innovation and consistency.[40]

Within this expansive cosmic narrative, we as humans are entrusted with authentic agency and freedom to write our individual stories within God's overarching story. We are not mere puppets reciting a preordained script. Though God sets pivotal milestones and outlines the broad trajectory of the storyline, we are invited to engage in a dynamic, 'faithful improvisation', exercising our divinely endowed freedoms and gifts in the cooperative dance between Word and Spirit that generates life and fosters community. Our responsibility lies in fully inhabiting this story, discerning our identity as God's people, and living out our purpose. To fulfil this, we need to immerse ourselves in the Spirit's movement within, through, and around us. Through the Spirit's unifying and diversifying work, we are incorporated into the life of Jesus Christ, and bonded with him and others. Yet, each of us plays a distinct role within his body, thus fulfilling our unique part in God's grand story of love.[41]

Charting a Narrative Course in Ecclesiology

The cumulative argument of this paper, which oscillates between biblical and systematic theologies while traversing from ecclesiology to hermeneutics and then back to ecclesiology, is designed with the following effect in mind: to present potential ways of enriching the current discourse on the church by proposing a narrative version of communion ecclesiology that takes seriously into consideration the fluid, biblically-shaped, and historically embedded nature of human involvement in the divine life. If properly articulated, this approach could offset the trend of crafting overly tidy, ahistorical, and romanticised depictions of the

---

40 N. T. Wright, "How Can the Bible be Authoritative? (The Laing Lecture for 1989)," *Vox Evangelica*, 21 (1991): 7-32. Accessed: https://ntwrightpage.com/2016/07/12/how-can-the-bible-be-authoritative/.

41 This ecclesiological vision is further developed in Lazic, *Towards an Adventist Version of Communio Ecclesiology*, 191-298.

church that overlook human failings, life's complexities, and current contextual realities.

I have proposed that biblical theology–with its emphasis on the storied nature of our universe and the narrative shape of God's revelation in Scripture–lays the fundamental groundwork for ecclesiological construction. While acknowledging that the church, as a profound mystery, remains not entirely comprehensible, this approach nevertheless guides our choice of a viable methodological path, mode of reasoning, and epistemic horizon. Furthermore, it enlightens our use of metaphors, marks, models, and other expressions when constructing an integrative vision of the church.

The rationale behind our proposal unfolds as follows: If Scripture is construed as an account 'revealing the movement of all things from God and their return into God', then communion ecclesiology, taking its cue from Scripture, must also follow the same narrative trajectory.[42] Rather than static or epic, the nature of this revelation is dramatic, mirroring the dynamism of our existence. Scripture is not merely a detached narrative but an evolving, forward-moving story that finds itself journeying along with history as an active player in this unfolding drama under the stewardship of the Spirit. The narrative revealed in Scripture is like a play authored by the Father, directed by the Spirit, with the Son as its chief actor. To comprehend our roles as individuals and as the church, we must position them within this primary drama of God. This grand narrative provides a reference point for all other reflections and informs the church's identity and mission.

Yet, still, we must acknowledge the intricacies that lie ahead in our ongoing endeavour of ecclesiological construction. Picture yourself suspended amidst the towering walls of various scholarly disciplines, each set apart, operating in secluded trenches. Instead of engaging in a vivacious, open-minded exchange–a dance of thought and discovery that is mutually enlightening and self-correcting–they stand siloed. This isolation deprives them of a more holistic and layered understanding of the divine-human communion. Rare voices daring to bridge the chasms between disciplines are too swiftly dismissed, their broad grasp deemed insufficient to grapple with the nuances and methodological demands within each separate realm. And so, rather than journeying in synergetic

---

42   Healy, 57.

dialogue, these disciplines remain solitary, failing to explore new intellectual landscapes that hold the promise of a more rounded vision of the mysteries of faith, or specifically, the communal Christian life. This state of affairs represents a profound missed opportunity, a lamentable failure to reach a greater depth of comprehension of the community-generative movement that draws humanity closer to their God.

It is within this interdisciplinary chasm that biblical theology could serve as a bridge. As a discipline, it not only magnifies and broadens the precise, detail-focused endeavours of biblical studies but also guides systematic theologians in their quest to articulate a cogent, compelling, and holistic vision that reverberates in an ever-shifting world. Simultaneously, it anchors the practical efforts of pastoral theologians, showcasing the transformative power of the lived experience of faith.

The potential of biblical theology, especially as articulated in recent decades, lies in its capacity to unify disparate and currently isolated disciplines. However, this field is complex and, at times, daunting. The challenge of navigating the myriad of intra-disciplinary requirements, methodological routes, and distinct norms and aspirations crafted within each respective discipline can feel akin to traversing a dangerous minefield. Despite good intentions and robust tactical preparation, missteps are inevitable, potentially leading to disaster. Hence, few dare to embark on this perilous journey. It seems safer to discuss faith's mysteries from a single angle within the secure walls of an established discipline. Yet, one cannot help but ponder–what is the cost of this safety?

Context, Issues and Future of Adventist Hermeneutics

Jan Barna

Introduction

The long-standing debate about the role of women in ministry has, more than anything else, led to surprisingly interpretative divisions in Adventism. Not only does Adventist theology not have a common mind on this matter, but worryingly the problem is symptomatic of the divide which exists in other areas, such as the view of Scripture, the doctrine of inspiration or how interpretation should operate generally. These are no minor concerns.

In this chapter, I intend to refer to the role of women in the gospel ministry debate as a useful and perhaps even necessary context since it is this debate more than any other which has revealed the contemporary Adventist approaches to interpretation.[1] However, in its analysis the chapter will foremost aim to scrutinize the hermeneutical issues of Adventist interpretation.

Right at the beginning it is important to clarify the main terminology relating to hermeneutics. This chapter uses 'hermeneutics' to delineate the theory which defines conditions of understanding between the reader and the text. As such the term 'hermeneutics' does not refer to exegetical procedures or techniques of interpretation–i.e. to 'biblical exegesis' as is traditionally understood to define

---

1   Such an analysis was the subject of my book which effectively is a study of Adventist hermeneutics. See Jan Barna, *Ordination of Women in Seventh-day Adventist Theology: A Study in Biblical Interpretations* (Preporod: Belgrade, 2012).

'methods'–but rather to a theory of how understanding is formed and what is involved in that. Specific interpretative methods, exegetical approaches or procedures are on a different–applied–level from hermeneutics. This chapter therefore maintains an essential notional difference between 'hermeneutics' and 'methods'. Additionally, the chapter will use the term 'interpretation' in a general sense to refer to a general field of interpretation without distinguishing between 'hermeneutics' and 'methods'.[2] Thus 'interpretation' is not equal to 'hermeneutics' and 'hermeneutics' is not synonymous with 'methods' or 'exegesis'.

The Context to Adventist Approaches

Adventist approaches to interpretation do not operate independently of the general field of biblical interpretation. Adventism was born in the time of the 19th-century revivalist evangelicalism in North America, and understandably it was influenced and shaped by the theoretical hermeneutical concerns of that time. To understand better–particularly regarding the context of modern Adventist approaches–it is valuable to introduce the field of biblical interpretation to serve as a contextual framework.

The subject of biblical hermeneutics has been evolving rapidly for the past 50 years. Particularly since the 1970s the world of evangelical interpretation[3]

---

[2] See, for example, Anthony C. Thiselton, *New Horizons in Hermeneutics: The Theory and Practice of Transforming Biblical Reading* (Grand Rapids: Zondervan, 1992), 48; or Anthony C. Thiselton, *A Concise Encyclopedia of the Philosophy of Religion* (Oxford: Oneworld Publications, 2002), 129 ('Hermeneutics denotes more than "rules for the interpretation of texts", even though it first emerged in this form.'). Also Alexander S. Jensen, *Theological Hermeneutics* (London: SCM, 2007), 2.

[3] The term 'evangelicalism' is almost impossibly elusive and notoriously difficult to define. This is not only because evangelicalism includes so many ecclesial traditions but also because these traditions are rooted in various historical and theological paradigms. Scholarly attempts to delineate kinds of evangelicalisms range from Webber's fourteen types to Hunter's four major types. See Robert E. Webber, *Common Roots: A Call to Evangelical Maturity* (Grand Rapids: Zondervan, 1979) and James Davison Hunter, American Evangelicalism: Conservative Religion and the Quandary of Modernity (New Brunswick, NJ: Rutgers University Press, 1983), 7-9. Garry Dorrien who distinguishes three types of evangelicalisms based on historical roots and then three types based on attitudes towards Scriptural authority, provides a useful introduction to evangelicalism. The three dominant paradigms in evangelical history are: Classical evangelicalism. This is grounded in the confessional and doctrinal heritage of the 16th-century Reformation, particularly the Reformed tradition.

to which Adventist approaches historically belong has diversified to the point where it can no longer be so easily defined. There are significant variations among various approaches to biblical interpretation in the contemporary scene.[4]

Worryingly for evangelical hermeneutics, some conservative evangelical textbooks on hermeneutics openly acknowledge that evangelicals have 'no common

---

Pietistic evangelicalism. The theological outlook of pietistic evangelicalism is on experience of conversion, sanctification, spiritual regeneration and healing, thus sharing the Puritan and Pietistic 18th-century concerns. Fundamentalist evangelicalism. The by-product of fundamentalist reaction against theological modernism. It emphasises absoluteness of certain fundamental beliefs that are denied by modern criticism. See Garry J. Dorrien, *The Remaking of Evangelical Theology* (Louisville, KY: Westminster John Knox, 1998), 1-11. If we take Dorrien's historical classification, it could be argued that Adventist ecclesial roots lie firmly within evangelicalism, particularly pietistic evangelicalism. It is therefore expected that its hermeneutical outlook will not be foreign to its evangelical roots.

4   For a definite discussion on the contemporary scene in biblical interpretation, see Anthony C. Thiselton, *The Two Horizons: New Testament Hermeneutics and Philosophical Description* (Carlisle: Paternoster, 1980); Anthony C. Thiselton, New Horizons in Hermeneutics (1992), Anthony C. Thiselton, *Thiselton on Hermeneutics: Collected Works with New Essays* (Aldershot: Ashgate, 2006) and Anthony C. Thiselton, *Hermeneutics: An Introduction* (Grand Rapids, MI/ Cambridge, UK: Eerdmans, 2009). Also prominent in the contemporary scene is the Scripture and Hermeneutics Series of which eight volumes have been published: Craig Bartholomew, Colin Greene and Karl Moller, eds., *Renewing Biblical Interpretation*. Scripture and Hermeneutics Series, Volume 1 (Carlisle: Paternoster, 2000); Craig Bartholomew, Colin Greene and Karl Moller, eds., *After Pentecost: Language and Biblical Interpretation*. Scripture and Hermeneutics Series, Volume 2 (Carlisle: Paternoster, 2001); Craig Bartholomew, Jonathan Chaplin, Robert Song and Al Wolters, eds., *A Royal Priesthood? A Use of the Bible Ethically and Politically, A Dialogue with Oliver O'Donovan*. Scripture and Hermeneutics Series, Volume 3 (Carlisle: Paternoster, 2002); Craig Bartholomew, Stephen C. Evans, Mary Healy and Murray Rae, eds., *'Behind' the Text: History and Biblical Interpretation*. Scripture and Hermeneutics Series, Volume 4 (Carlisle: Paternoster, 2003); Craig Bartholomew, Mary Healy, Karl Moller and Robin Parry, eds., *Out of Egypt: Biblical Theology and Biblical Interpretation*. Scripture and Hermeneutics Series, Volume 5 (Milton Keynes: Paternoster, 2004); Craig G. Bartholomew, Joel B. Green and Anthony C. Thiselton, eds., *Reading Luke: Interpretation, Reflection, Formation*. Scripture and Hermeneutics Series, Volume 6 (Milton Keynes: Paternoster, 2005); Craig Bartholomew, Scott Hahn, Robin Parry, Christopher Seitz and Al Wolters, eds., *Canon and Biblical Interpretation*. Scripture and Hermeneutics Series, Volume 7 (Milton Keynes: Paternoster, 2006) and David Lyle Jeffrey and Stephen C. Evans, eds., *The Bible and the University*. Scripture and Hermeneutics Series, Volume 8 (Milton Keynes: Paternoster, 2007). A very useful overview of past and present hermeneutical approaches is also in Gerald

mind' on most issues.⁵ Given the evolving and progressively diverse nature of the field of biblical hermeneutics, I would suggest that a way to approach it constructively is through organising the discussion within the categories of traditional/classical, new/modern and neo-pragmatic/context-relative hermeneutics.⁶

The traditional or classical interpretation is characterised by its fixation on the text and its historical worlds. In essence, a text-centered interpretation uses methodological approaches utilising technical tools appropriate to dealing with the text and its background. Traditionally, therefore, this interpretation is oriented on particular rules and procedures. Notably, this approach does not raise naturally deeper questions about hermeneutical theory which arise primarily from the reader's perspective.⁷

The new or modern hermeneutics on the other hand is characterised by its multidisciplinary focus which demands a respect for contingency and the particularity of the interpretative task. Hence, particular interpretative procedures of particular readers as they read particular genres and particular texts is considered multidisciplinary hermeneutics. At the heart of such approach/es is, however, a basic recognition that not only does the horizon of the text need be taken into consideration, but also the reader's ability to shape the understanding. Notably, this approach is more prone to raising hermeneutical issues,

---

Bray, *Biblical Interpretation*: Past and Present (Downers Grove, IL: InterVarsity, 1996) or Stanley E. Porter and Beth M. Stovell, eds. *Biblical Hermeneutics*: Five Views (Downers Grove, IL: IVP Academic, 2012).

5   Gerald Bray, *Biblical Interpretation*, 542. See also pages 465 and 476-7.
6   See for example Anthony C. Thiselton, *Thiselton on Hermeneutics*, 393.
7   While I will further characterise traditional hermeneutics in the following pages, the main representative sources of this approach could be identified with Bernard Ramm, *Protestant Biblical Interpretation: A Textbook of Hermeneutics*, 3rd revised ed., (Grand Rapids: Baker Books, 1970); Gordon D. Fee, *To What End Exegesis? Essays Textual, Exegetical, and Theological* (Grand Rapids: Eerdmans, 2001), *New Testament Exegesis: A Handbook for Students and Pastors*, 3rd revised ed., (Louisville, KY: Westminster John Knox Press, 2002), with Douglass Stuart, *How to Read the Bible for All its Worth: A Guide to Understanding the Bible*, 2nd ed., (New York: Zondervan, 2003); Walter Kaiser and Moises Silva, *An Introduction to Biblical Hermeneutics*, (New York: Zondervan, 1994); E. D. Hirsch, *Validity in Interpretation*, (New Haven: Yale University Press, 1967), *The Aims of Interpretation* (Chicago: University of Chicago Press, 1976) or Milton S. Terry, *Biblical Hermeneutics: A Treatise on the Interpretation of the Old and New Testaments* (Grand Rapids: Zondervan, 1961 [1890]) in the 19th and early 20th century.

arising from its attention to the reader's horizon, such as the function of language, understanding and pre-understanding and theory of meaning.[8]

The neo-pragmatic or context-relative interpretation could be seen as the opposite approach to the traditional model-oriented approach. The neo-pragmatic interpretation takes the positive affirmation of the reader's contribution that is acknowledged by modern hermeneutics and applies it in its absolute sense. Thus the meaning is understood to be always relative to the reader or a community of readers. The reader-relative and pragmatic nature of this approach is visible in its main question which is not 'what does it mean?' but rather 'what does it do?' The key sentence that captures the essence of neo-pragmatic hermeneutics is: 'The reader's response is not to the meaning; it is the meaning.'[9]

Within such a subjectivist theoretical model as neo-pragmatic context-relative hermeneutics creates, the meaning effectively does not correct the readers and no prophetic voice is heard beyond the limited interest fields of the readers.

Since the neo-pragmatic approaches in their essence defeat the purpose of biblical interpretation, I will in the following consider only the traditional and modern hermeneutics that are more relevant to the evangelical and Adventist contexts. In general terms, Adventist interpretation arising from its larger evangelical context can be identified with the traditional approaches as opposed to what is today called new or modern hermeneutics.[10]

---

8   The multidisciplinary nature of hermeneutics that takes into consideration metacritical questions of hermeneutical theory is best represented by the work of Anthony C. Thiselton. See, for example, *The New Horizons in Hermeneutics*.
9   Stanley E. Fish, *Is there a Text in this Class? The Authority of Interpretive Communities* (Cambridge: Harvard University Press, 1980), 3, cf 1-17. Italics original.
10 For a detailed discussion on the difference between traditional hermeneutics and new hermeneutics see Anthony C. Thiselton, *Thiselton on Hermeneutics*, chapters 25 and 26 (441-61 and 463-48). By 'new hermeneutic' here I do not mean just the particular school of thought of Ebeling, Fuchs and Bultmann, but a general new trend which considers the problems of the reader's perspective and not just the textual horizon. On the particular school of new hermeneutic of Ebeling, Fuchs and Bultmann see, for example, James M. Robinson and John B. Cobb, Jr., ed. *New Frontiers in Theology: Discussion among Continental and American Theologians*, Volume II: The New Hermeneutic (New York: Harper & Row, 1964).

Elements of Traditional and Modern Hermeneutics

Probably the main distinguishing characteristics between the traditional and new schools are the various emphases each school puts either on the text or the reader. While traditional interpretation is predominantly concerned with the text and develops its interpretative strategies in the form of rules and principles of interpretation (exegesis) around the text, new hermeneutics recognises the importance of the reader in the hermeneutical process and hence it develops approaches arising from hermeneutical theory which involves a reflection about the reader's problems, namely the problems of pre-understanding, understanding and language.

The difference between traditional model-oriented interpretation and modern hermeneutical theory-oriented interpretation can be illustrated by the way each defines hermeneutics. Traditional evangelical definitions of hermeneutics tend almost univocally to emphasise that 'hermeneutics' is a study of rules and principles of interpretation.[11] On the other hand, definitions of modern hermeneutics speak of the subject in terms of reflection on the conditions of understanding.[12]

This initial comparison of traditional and modern fields of interpretation can be further elaborated by highlighting the following elements of traditional interpretation: 1. Text-centred intentionalism, 2. A two-stage approach, 3. Methodology of rules and principles, 4. Negligence of the reader's horizon and 5. The lack of theoretical considerations.

1. Text-Centred Intentionalism

Behind the intentionalism of traditional hermeneutics is intentionalism in its evangelical Hirschian form. The key characteristic of evangelical intentionalism is a belief that exegetical work of textual analysis will yield a fixed or unchanging meaning which the text contains. For E.D. Hirsch the meaning is the same as the

---

11 For example: Bernard Ramm, *Protestant Biblical Interpretation*, 1 or William W. Klein, Craig L. Blomberg and Robert L. Hubbard, Jr., *Introduction to Biblical Interpretation*, Revised and Expanded, (Nashville, TN: Thomas Nelson, 2004), 5.

12 Alexander S. Jensen, *Theological Hermeneutics*, 2. Anthony C. Thiselton, *New Horizons in Hermeneutics*, 48. Also Anthony C. Thiselton, *A Concise Encyclopedia of the Philosophy of Religion*, 129.

author's intention and can be recovered from the text.[13] Thus traditional hermeneutics believes in the possibility of recovering the original meaning or intention of the author from the text with the help of appropriate exegetical procedures.[14]

Given the wide historical and cultural gap between the present-day reader and the author, intentionalist hermeneutics conceives of the meaning as being somehow trapped inside a lifeless body of the text, awaiting revival and liberation through the use of the right methodology. The historical gap is indeed viewed in traditional hermeneutics as a desert through which the reader must travel to uncover the fresh fountain of meaning.[15] Traditional hermeneutics thus never deviates from the text within which the meaning is trapped.

For such a text-centred intentionalism of classical hermeneutics, the utilisation of 'objective' exegetical rules and strategies becomes absolutely vital for the successful recovering of the original meaning. A right methodology becomes for traditional hermeneutics not only the guarantee of correct interpretation but also a critical aspect of its mindset. It will come as no surprise, then, that the

---

13   E. D. Hirsch in *Validity in Interpretation*, on page 8 writes regarding the meaning: 'It is what the author meant by his use of a particular sign sequence.' For an Evangelical exploration of the Hirschian intentionalism see Walter C. Kaiser and Moises Silva, *An Introduction to Biblical Hermeneutics*, particularly 27-45.
14   For example, Gordon Fee, 'History as Context for Interpretation', in *The Acts of Bible Reading*, ed. Elmer Dyck (Downers Grove, IL: InterVarsity, 1996); and Walter Kaiser, *Towards an Exegetical Theology: Biblical Exegesis for Preaching and Teaching* (Grand Rapids: Baker Academic, 1981).
15   Roger Lundin, 'Interpreting Orphans: Hermeneutics in the Cartesian Tradition', in *The Promise of Hermeneutics*, Roger Lundin, Clarence Walhout and Anthony C. Thiselton (Carlisle: Paternoster, 1999), 41 and 55. For an analysis of intentionalism see pages 36-41. The problem with the intentionalist approach to hermeneutics is that, as Lundin argues, it reflects the cold and soulless Cartesian philosophy of first-person certainty. However, as Roger Scruton concludes in his analysis of Descartian philosophy, 'the assumption that there is a first-person certainty ... has been finally removed from the centre of philosophy'; Roger Scruton, *From Descartes to Wittgenstein: A Short History of Modern Philosophy* (New York: Harper & Row, 1981), 284. Intentionalism in its Hirschian form thus 'stands pretty much by [itself] in the landscape of contemporary critical theory', as Frank Lentricchia observes in his analysis of Hirschian intentionalism. See Frank Lentricchia, *After the New Criticism* (Chicago: University of Chicago Press, 1980), 257.

interpretative goal for traditional hermeneutics is to recover the original historical meaning or, as K. J. Vanhoozer calls it, a 'determinative textual meaning'.[16]

2. A two-stage approach

The second methodological characteristic of evangelical hermeneutics is what can be called the two-stage approach to interpretation. While the discussion so far has pointed out that recovering the original meaning is the objective of hermeneutics, it is nevertheless not the sole goal of the evangelical interpretation. Traditional hermeneutics has in fact a dual objective. The first is to secure the historical meaning by means of exegesis. But the interpretation has not fulfilled its purpose until this exegetically secured unchanging meaning is applied to the present-day reader's situation. Hence traditional evangelical hermeneutics proceeds in two stages to reach its objectives. The historical-textual analysis uncovers the original meaning while the second stage of application is concerned with the original meaning's significance for today. The methodology was first introduced by Schleiermacher and later popularised by E. D. Hirsch and Gordon D. Fee in evangelical biblical studies.[17]

3. Methodology of rules and principles

The strong emphasis on the methodology of rules and principles is another good indicator of traditional hermeneutics. This emphasis is central to evangelical interpretation. Almost without exception the major traditional Protestant books on interpretation are primarily explorations of various methods and principles of interpretation. As examples of this trend can be mentioned the classical

---

16 William W. Klein, Craig L. Blomberg and Robert L. Hubbard, Jr., *Introduction to Biblical Interpretation*, 18-19 and 153; and K. J. Vanhoozer, *Is There a Meaning in This Text? The Bible, the Reader, and the Morality of Knowledge* (Grand Rapids: Zondervan, 1998), 300.

17 Schleiermacher's approach consisted of (a) objective historical-linguistic investigation and (b) a psychological step in which one has to learn more about the author. While retaining the two-stage approach, the evangelicals nevertheless modified it somewhat to (a) the objective exegetical step which secures the unchanging meaning and (b) the subjective appropriation of the significance of the text which applies it to a present-day situation. It has been especially Hirsch's *Validity in Interpretation* and Fee's work which have been influential on evangelical biblical studies. See Roger Lundin, 'Interpreting Orphans: Hermeneutics in the Cartesian Tradition', in *The Promise of Hermeneutics*, 36-38.

influential work of Bernard Ramm, *Protestant Biblical Interpretation*, as well as the equally influential and comprehensive hermeneutical textbook by William Klein and his co-authors, *Introduction to Biblical Hermeneutics*, or Walter C. Kaiser and Moises Silva's *An Introduction to Biblical Hermeneutics* and perhaps Louis Berkhof's *Principles of Biblical Interpretation*. All these can be taken as representatives of the classical text-oriented evangelical Protestant approach to biblical hermeneutics.

It is illuminating to observe how much emphasis these representative sources place on the correct methodology which is defined in terms of a set of rules and principles of interpretation. For example, for Berkhof 'hermeneutics is the science that teaches us the principles, laws, and methods of interpretation'.[18] William Klein, Craig Blomberg and Robert Hubbard, in their *Introduction to Biblical Interpretation*, set the basic goal of their book to be in establishing 'guidelines and methods to guide those who want to understand Scripture correctly'. They claim the readers need an approach of methods or 'agreed-upon principles' which are the best guarantee for correct interpretation.[19] Given the prominence of right methods and rules in Protestant hermeneutics, it could be said that Protestant biblical scholarship reduces hermeneutics to mere exegesis.[20]

Closely related to the methodology of rules and principles is the notion of 'method' as such. With regard to the analysis of Adventist approaches, it may be worth noting the variety of names which traditional Protestant hermeneutics gives to its method. The most preferred names appear to be 'philological', 'historical', 'grammatical' or 'historical-grammatical' or even 'critical'. All these terminologies are not alien to evangelical vocabulary and, as Bernard Ramm

---

18 Louis Berkhof, *Principles of Biblical Interpretation* (Grand Rapids: Baker Books, 1975), 11.
19 William W. Klein, Craig L. Blomberg and Robert L. Hubbard, Jr., *Introduction to Biblical Interpretation*, 5. Moreover, they also define hermeneutics in line with other evangelical scholars as 'both a science and an art' (see page 5).
20 William W. Klein, Craig L. Blomberg and Robert L. Hubbard, Jr. in *Introduction to Biblical Interpretation* on page 20 argue that: 'Proper hermeneutics provides the conceptual framework for interpreting correctly by means of accurate exegesis. Exegesis puts into practice one's theory of interpretation. Thus good hermeneutics will generate good exegetical methods.'

argues, all of these could be used as valid descriptions of the traditional evangelical methodology or interpretation.[21]

4. Negligence of the Reader's Horizon

Traditional hermeneutics—as opposed to modern hermeneutics—is not concerned with developing relevant concepts of language, meaning, the reader's understanding and pre-understanding or a theory of the role of the reader as such, as does modern hermeneutical theory. Traditional interpretation is exclusively preoccupied with the horizon of the text only and it leaves out the reader's perspective from the hermeneutical considerations.[22] One may argue that it is not discussing hermeneutics as such, but rather only exegetical methods which scrutinise the text and its world.

5. Lack of Concern for Hermeneutical Theory

The ignorance of the reader's horizon and the consequent lack of concern for hermeneutical theory of the traditional approaches have been also pointed out from inside traditional evangelical scholarship. Julius Scott and Walter Kaiser in particular raised questions as early as 1979 about the sleeping condition of traditional evangelical scholarship with regard to the consideration of hermeneutical theory. Scott observes that 'for many evangelical Christians, hermeneutics is an area whose importance is granted but whose nature and content is little understood'.[23] Indeed, the attention of the majority of evangelical scholarship in and before the 1970s was on inerrancy and inspiration debates, and before the 1980s

---

21   Bernard Ramm, *Protestant Biblical Interpretation*, 114. Ramm mentions philological, historical, grammatical or historical-grammatical, or even critical method as valid descriptions of Protestant biblical method. The comprehensive volume of Klein and his colleagues also favours the historical-grammatical name for their preferred method. See William W. Klein, Craig L. Blomberg and Robert L. Hubbard, Jr., Introduction to Biblical Interpretation, 13.

22   The concept of horizon was introduced into hermeneutics by Gadamer. See Hans-Georg Gadamer, *Truth and Method* (London: Continuum, 2004), 300-305. Both the text and the reader have their horizons. See also Alexander S. Jensen, *Theological Hermeneutics*, 139-42. Traditional hermeneutics uses the word 'presupposition' instead of 'horizon of expectation' which is preferred by hermeneutical theoreticians. On how 'horizons of expectation' function see, for example, Anthony C. Thiselton, *New Horizons in Hermeneutics*, 44-46.

23   Julius J. Scott, Jr., 'Some Problems in Hermeneutics for Contemporary Evangelicals', *Journal of the Evangelical Theological Society*, 22 (1979): 67.

hermeneutics was treated with a rather indifferent attitude.[24] Walter Kaiser even goes as far as to say that 'much of the current debate over the Scriptures ... is, at its core, a result of failure on the part of evangelicals to come to terms with the issue of hermeneutics'.[25]

The observations of both Scott and Kaiser are important for understanding the present and the historical position of traditional evangelical hermeneutics. Since traditional evangelical hermeneutics has been up until recent decades preoccupied primarily with the inspiration and inerrancy debates which have been part of the larger evangelical concern for biblical authority, it may be advantageous to see such concerns as important aspects of traditional hermeneutics.

Inspiration and Authority of Scripture Concerns

Historically, the doctrine of Scripture and its authority occupied a central place in the Protestant system of interpretation. This aspect had become even more prominent at the time of the emergence of liberal Protestantism in the 19th century.[26] Particularly the Princeton theologians such as Archibald Alexander, Charles Hodge, Archibald Hodge and Benjamin Warfield launched a decisive attack against the liberal view of Scripture and in doing so set the agenda for evangelicals for many decades to come.[27] Evangelical authors on hermeneutics such as Gerald Bray had singled out Benjamin B. Warfield (1851-1921) as one of the key influential persons for the modern evangelical doctrine of Scripture. It can be argued that for Warfield, the Bible (a) is verbally inspired, though in

---

24　John R. Muether, 'Evangelicals and the Bible: A Bibliographic Postscript', in *Inerrancy and Hermeneutic: A Tradition, A Challenge, A Debate*, ed. Harvie M. Conn (Grand Rapids: Baker Books, 1988), 253-64.

25　Walter C. Kaiser, Jr., 'Legitimate Hermeneutics,' in *Inerrancy*, ed. Norman L. Geisler (Grand Rapids: Zondervan, 1980), 117.

26　Ronald Satta, a defender of Christian Fundamentalism, has put forward a proposition in which he argues that the doctrine of the high view of Scripture (absolute inerrancy view) has been the central doctrine of Protestantism from its very beginning. Satta also maintains that the core of Fundamentalism does not lie in the doctrine of eschatology but in its doctrine of Scripture, precisely a high view of Scripture. Ronald F. Satta, *The Sacred Text: Biblical Authority in Nineteenth-Century America*, Princeton Theological Monograph Series 73 (Eugene, OR: Pickwick Publications, 2007), 103, footnote 11.

27　Mark A. Noll, *The Princeton Theology: 1812-1921* (Grand Rapids: Baker Books, 1983).

a less mechanical or immediate way than normally asserted,[28] (b) it is factually inerrant in everything it mentions including historical or scientific details and (c) only the autographs were without any error and hence inspired.[29]

Warfield was the first one who had limited the qualifications of inerrancy to the category of original autographs, even though after him many other qualifications have been added.[30] Nonetheless, evangelicals appear to have maintained unanimity regarding their views of biblical authority.[31] Warfield in this regard is still seen as probably the key figure in shaping the evangelical doctrine of Scripture and its inspiration.[32]

Warfield's teaching in modern dress was, for example, expounded by the International Council on Biblical Inerrancy in its so-called Chicago Statement (1978). The summary section of the document contains five central statements: About the truthfulness of God (point 1), infallibility in all matters upon which Scripture touches (point 2), the Spirit's illumination (point 3), verbal

---

28 The view of Scripture based on immediate activity of God means that the Holy Spirit inspired the Bible through immediate activity, with human agents being rather inactive. On the other hand, the mediate view of Scripture allows human agents to mediate what they receive or experience under inspiration. Kern Trembath's work *Evangelical Theories of Biblical Inspiration: A Review and Proposal* (Oxford: Oxford University Press, 1987), based on his doctoral research, has demonstrated that a tension between mediate and immediate positions had been present particularly in Warfield's view of Scripture. While Trembath shows how Hodge, Warfield or Montgomery's theories of Scripture are similar in their Common Sense Philosophy assumptions, the deductivist methodology they follow and the absolute inerrancy conclusions they reach, it is particularly Warfield's view of Scripture's inspiration that is neither mediate nor fully immediate. See Kern R. Trembath, Evangelical Theories of Biblical Inspiration, 8-46. Warfield's position is explored on pages 20-27.

29 Gerald Bray, *Biblical Interpretation*, 555-559.

30 Morris Ashcraft, 'Revelation and Biblical Authority in Eclipse', *Faith and Mission*, Spring 1987, 10.

31 Carl F. Henry's, *God, Revelation and Authority*, 6 vols. (Waco, TX: Word, 1976-1983) could well be regarded as the magnum opus of evangelicalism. Different types of inerrancy concepts held by evangelicals are discussed, for example, in Robert K. Johnston, Evangelicals at an Impasse: Biblical Authority in Practice (Atlanta, GA: John Knox Press, 1979); Robert McNair Price, 'The Crisis of Biblical Authority: The Setting and Range of the Current Evangelical Crisis', (PhD dissertation, Drew University, 1981), 99-243 and Clark C. Pinnock, 'Evangelicals and Inerrancy: The Current Debate', *Theology Today*, 35, 1978, 66-67.

32 From within Adventist scholarship Peter M. van Bemmelen has, for example, assessed the contribution of Warfield's inspiration theory. See his 'Issues in Biblical Inspiration: Sanday and Warfield', (ThD dissertation, Andrews University, 1987), especially 197-309.

inspiration and inerrancy in all its teaching (point 4) and an all-or-nothing position regarding the divine authority of Scripture if the full inerrancy is downgraded to limited inerrancy (point 5).[33]

It is important to notice how prominent and central these inspiration-revelation and biblical authority concerns were for the traditional evangelical outlook. According to Scott and Kaiser this fixation on such concerns led to the neglect of deeper hermeneutical questions.[34] The theoretical base–i.e. the hermeneutics–of traditional interpretation was thus narrowed down to inspiration-revelation discussion and biblical authority affirmation.

Common-Sense and the Baconian Heritage of Traditional Text-Oriented Hermeneutics

So far we have delineated traditional hermeneutics in terms of five aspects: text-centeredness; the two-stage approach of exegesis and application; methodology of rules and guidelines for reading; negligence of the reader's horizon and a general lack of concern for hermeneutical theory and concerns for the inspiration of Scripture. Equally important as touching on the key aspects may,

---

33 The Chicago statement on Biblical Inerrancy was first published in toto including its 'Summary Statements', 'Articles of Affirmation and Denial' and 'Exposition' by C. F. H. Henry in *God, Revelation and Authority*, vol. 4 (Waco, TX: Word, 1979), 211-19. The statement was signed by more than 300 leading evangelical scholars, among them James Boice, Norman L. Geisler, Carl F. H. Henry, Harold Lindsell, John Warwick Montgomery, J. I. Packer, Francis Schaeffer, R. C. Sproul and John Wenham.

34 However, in recent decades the perception in the contemporary field of evangelical hermeneutics is slowly changing towards recognition of the importance of hermeneutical theory thanks especially to a leading hermeneutical theoretician, Anthony C. Thiselton, who is working from within evangelical scholarship. Especially influential were Thiselton's *Two Horizons* (1980) and *New Horizons* (1992). Among his recent contributions is his volume containing a collection of his essays, including new essays *Thiselton on Hermeneutics* (2006) and *Hermeneutics of Doctrine* (2007). Robert Knowles' recent PhD dissertation also assesses Thiselton's work as being unique and groundbreaking in the field of hermeneutics. See Robert Knowles, 'The Grammar of Hermeneutics: Anthony C. Thiselton and the Search for a Unified Theory' (PhD thesis, Cardiff University, 2005) later published as Robert Knowles, *Anthony C. Thiselton and the Grammar of Hermeneutics: A Search for a Unified Theory* (Milton Keynes, UK: Paternoster, 2012).

however, be to briefly introduce the historical-theoretical heritage of traditional hermeneutics.

For most of their history, evangelicals–especially in America–have denied that they had a philosophy. All they were doing, they thought, was using their common sense and following Sola Scriptura. However, the evangelical world has been awakening to the fact that their thinking had been shaped by philosophical forces more than they were willing to acknowledge: a significant impact had been made on modern evangelicalism and their hermeneutics, particularly by the Scottish Common Sense Philosophy and the American Didactic Enlightenment.[35]

Scottish Common Sense philosophy derives its roots from the teachings of Thomas Reid (1710-1796). Reid was a contemporary of David Hume whose skeptical empiricism Reid wanted to overcome. Hume insisted that humans do not perceive things that are external, but only certain images and pictures of them imprinted upon the mind.[36] This way, observers cannot know for sure whether what they perceive corresponds to the real world that exists outside of sensory perceptions. Empirical observers cannot even know whether they can rely on their senses which in fact may or may not transmit the outside world to their mind accurately.[37]

Against such skeptical empiricist philosophy (which Reid believed threatened not only the foundations of scientific explorations but also the foundations of Christian faith), Reid responded with his philosophy of direct realism. Central to Reid's thought is what he calls the 'principles of common sense'. Such principles are used and presupposed by all human beings. It was in fact God, the Supreme Being that governs the world by the laws of nature, who also furnished the human mind with basic dispositions so that 'every man of common

---

35 Mark A. Noll, *The Scandal of the Evangelical Mind* (Grand Rapids, MI and Cambridge, UK: William B. Eerdmans Publishing Company, 1994), 83-88.
36 David Hume, *A Treatise on Human Nature*, ed. L. A. Selby-Bigge, 2nd ed. revised by P. H. Nidditch (Oxford: Clarendon, 1978), 1.1.
37 A concise introduction to Hume's philosophy in relation to Christian thought is provided by Colin Brown, *Christianity and Western Thought: A History of Philosophers, Ideas and Movements*. Volume 1: From the Ancient World to the Age of Enlightenment (Downers Grove: InterVarsity, 1990), 234-58. For an extensive bibliography on Hume and his work, see Brown's note 1 on page 402.

understanding ... finds it absolutely necessary to conduct his actions and opinions by them.'[38]

Because God is the author of both the laws of nature and the principles of common sense, a direct correspondence exists between the mind and empirical reality. Reid's central hypothesis, therefore, in essence proposes that God has tuned into the human mind of each person in such a way that it is able to read the physical world accurately almost by default. All that observers then need to do is to collect all available data from a studied field by the method of induction and the truth will become apparent to the mind. This way Reid and his followers were able to overcome the reader's problem which effectively Hume had raised.

The ideas of Scottish Common Sense Realism in America, combined with Baconian and Newtonian scientific methods based on inductive collecting and combining data, created what Mark Noll calls the 'American Didactic Enlightenment' or 'Evangelical Enlightenment.'[39] The American Enlightenment provided just the right tools to enable evangelicals to master the tumults of the philosophically and politically revolutionary era of the 18th and 19th centuries. Nowhere was the marriage between evangelically minded Protestantism, Scottish Common Sense Realism and inductive scientific Baconianism more visible than in the doctrine of Scripture.

Baconian inductive methodology and the assumptions of Common Sense philosophy meant that evangelicals began to treat Scripture as a scientific text whose pieces were to be collected and arranged, and the reader would then in an almost obvious manner recognise the truths on any issue. In 1859 a Restorationist, James Lamar, summarised these sentiments well:

> *The Scriptures admit of being studied and expounded upon the principles of the inductive method; and ... when thus interpreted they speak to us in a voice as certain and unmistakable as the language of nature heard in the experiments and observations of science.*[40]

---

38 Thomas Reid, *Essays on Intellectual Powers of Man*, 1.2. For an extensive bibliography on Thomas Reid's work, see Colin Brown, *Christianity and Western Thought*, note 1 on pages 405-406.
39 Mark A. Noll, *The Scandal of the Evangelical Mind*, 87-88.
40 James S. Lamar, *Organon of Scripture; or, The Inductive Method of Biblical Interpretation* (1859), quoted in Richard T. Hughes and Leonard C. Allen, *Illusions of Innocence: Protestant Primitivism in America*, 1630-1875 (Chicago:

It is therefore noteworthy that the Bible became 'a store-house of facts' and its nature understood in a propositional sense.[41] The virtues of objectivity, scientific precision and trust in the capacities of the common sense (mind) of the reader are the defining traits of evangelical hermeneutical thought.

By way of summary, if hermeneutics can be classified as a species occupying the middle ground between epistemology and methodology, as Alexander Jensen argues,[42] then hermeneutics should not only be concerned with developing a right set of guidelines for interpreting texts but also be informed by a theory of knowledge about what is involved when readers attempt to understand texts. A visible lack of theoretical reflection concerning the reader's perspective is an aspect of traditional hermeneutics which may be open to discussion.

The Place of Adventist Approaches within the Field of Biblical Interpretation

Given Adventism's historical and theological roots, its interpretative approaches largely belong to the world of evangelical tradition.[43]

With some simplification we can argue that the most visible distinguishing characteristic between the traditional and new schools is the various emphases each school puts either on the text or the reader. While traditional hermeneutics is predominantly concerned with the text and develops its interpretative strategies in the form of exegetical rules around the text, new approaches to hermeneutics more readily recognise the importance of the reader's perspective in the hermeneutical process of creating understanding.[44]

University of Chicago Press, 1988), 156-57 and 161. Leonard Woods' sentiments (1822) about the best method of Bible study, '[one] which is perused in the science of physics' , regulated 'by the maxims of Bacon and Newton' , were quite common among evangelicals. See Leonard Woods, quoted in Herbert Hovenkamp, Science and Religion in America, 1800-1860 (Philadelphia: University of Pennsylvania Press, 1978), 61.

41 Charles Hodge, *Systematic Theology*, 3 vols. (Grand Rapids: Eerdmans, 1952 [orig. 1872-73]), 1:10-11.

42 Alexander S. Jensen, *Theological Hermeneutics*, 5-6.

43 See Garry J. Dorrien, *The Remaking of Evangelical Theology*, 1-11. If we take Dorrien's historical classification, it could be argued that Adventist ecclesial roots lie firmly within evangelicalism, particularly pietistic evangelicalism.

44 Traditional hermeneutics is defined as 'the science that teaches us the principles, laws, and methods of interpretation'. See Louis Berkhof, *Principles of Biblical Interpretation*, 11. Given the emphasis on methods and rules in

The text-centred intentionalism, the methodology of rules and principles and a two-stage approach to exegesis and application are the most visible aspects of traditional hermeneutics. In addition, a strong concern for the inspiration and authority of Scripture and the underdeveloped concerns for the reader's horizon lead to underestimation of theoretical matters. Adventist interpretative approaches, past and present and of various theological convictions, tend to reflect all these above-mentioned aspects.

Intentionalist assumptions, for example, are particularly visible in the way the representatives of ordination of women camps treat individual biblical texts and passages. While for the opponents the meaning is assumed to be present in the text in a literal, plain, natural and direct form, for the proponents the meaning is found in the text more indirectly in the form of principles.[45] Behind both these views, however, there is a noticeable assumption of intentionalism, especially intentionalism in its traditional evangelical Hirschian form.[46]

The key characteristic of such traditional intentionalism is a belief that exegetical work of textual analysis will yield a fixed or unchanging meaning which the text contains. Adventist interpretation also assumes similar functioning of biblical texts where the meaning is present in the form of the authorial intention.

Gerhard Hasel's reference to the work of E. D. Hirsch and Walter Keiser as the benchmark for evangelical biblical hermeneutics can probably be used as an indicative example. Hasel's intentionalist view is evident from the direct appeal to Kaiser's statement: 'To interpret, we must in every case reproduce the sense the

---

Protestant hermeneutics, it could be said that Protestant biblical scholarship, reduces hermeneutics to mere exegesis. See William W. Klein, Craig L. Blomberg and Robert L. Hubbard Jr. *Introduction to Biblical Interpretation* on page 20: 'Proper hermeneutics provides the conceptual framework for interpreting correctly by means of accurate exegesis. Exegesis puts into practice one's theory of interpretation. Thus good hermeneutics will generate good exegetical methods.' Modern hermeneutics, on the other hand, sees the nature and the task of interpretation differently. See Alexander S. Jensen, *Theological Hermeneutics*, 2.

45   See, for example, Holmes's argumentation in Mercedes H. Dyer, ed., *Prove All Things: A Response to Women in Ministry* (Berrien Springs, MI: Adventist Affirm, 2000), 163.
46   For Hirsch the correct meaning could be found in the author's intention which can be recovered from the text. E. D. Hirsch in *Validity in Interpretation* writes regarding the meaning: 'It is what the author meant by his use of a particular sign sequence' (see page 8).

Scriptural writer intended for his own words.'[47] Moreover Adventist interpreters believe in the possibility and necessity of recovering the original meaning or the intention of the author from the text with the help of appropriate exegetical procedures just as classical evangelical hermeneutics does.[48]

(2) For such a text-centred intentionalism of classical hermeneutics, using 'objective' exegetical rules and strategies becomes absolutely vital for successfully recovering the original meaning which lies on the other side of the cultural and historical abyss.[49]

Viewed from this perspective, for example, the debate between Adventist proponents and opponents of women's ministry concerning the correct, objective or scientific methodology provides clear indications of their traditional hermeneutics.

While it is true that Adventist opponents have a tendency to overlook or marginalise the historical gap in their method, this cannot be taken as evidence of their lack of commitment to a method, let alone intentionalism. In fact both their and also proponents' views about the meaning which is often referred to as 'timeless truth' or 'universal principle(s)', coupled with following a detailed rules-and-principles strategy to recover the 'changeless' truths, are clear evidences of intentionalist thinking and commitment to a methodology of rules and principles.[50] All these examples place Adventist interpretation within the framework of traditional hermeneutics which is characterised by its

---

47   Gerhard Hasel, 'Biblical Authority, Hermeneutics, and the Role of Women,' Commission on the Role of Women unpublished paper, 1998, 6. Kaiser's statement is from Walter C. Kaiser, 'Legitimate Hermeneutics', in *Inerrancy*, 118.
48   For example, Gordon Fee, 'History as Context for Interpretation', in *The Acts of Bible Reading*; and Walter Kaiser, *Towards an Exegetical Theology*.
49   Roger Lundin, 'Interpreting Orphans: Hermeneutics in the Cartesian Tradition', in *The Promise of Hermeneutics*, 41 and 55. For an analysis of intentionalism, see pages 36-41.
50   See especially opponents' and proponents' sets of rules of interpretation. Both sets of rules demonstrate strong exegetical commitment to recover the 'truth' from the texts. It could even be argued that the opponents' case rests on the assumption that the disputed texts contain universally binding and therefore unchanging truths which can be recovered by literalistic reading. On the other hand, the proponents' principle-based reading of the texts also strongly assumes that the meaning can be revived in the form of eternal principles which can be formulated with the help of textual-historical analysis.

text-centeredness, intentionalism and reliance on a methodology based on exegetical rules and principles.

Furthermore, the third main aspect of evangelical hermeneutics, i.e. a two-part exegesis and application approach to interpretation, is also a visible trait of Adventist approaches.[51]

Particularly the proponents' interpretation distinguishes carefully between the two methodological steps of historical, cultural and linguistic exegesis and application. This is, for example, visible in the way proponents define the nature of interpretation as being both a science and an art.[52] For proponents, the science part of the definition refers to exegetical procedures, often argued to be objective and scientific, while the art part in the definitions refers to subjective appropriation of what exegesis discovers.

Equally, a similar two-step model of interpretation is visible in the opponents' approaches.[53] Gerhard Hasel back in the 1980s directly approved of the Hirschian two-stage approach of 'meaning' and 'significance' as the correct method of interpretation.[54]

---

51 I have indicated in the introduction that the two-part methodology was first introduced by Schleiermacher and later popularised by E. D. Hirsch and Gordon D. Fee in evangelical biblical studies. See Roger Lundin, 'Interpreting Orphans: Hermeneutics in the Cartesian Tradition' , in *The Promise of Hermeneutics*, 36-38. It has been especially Hirsch's *Validity in Interpretation* (1967) and Fee's work which have been influential in evangelical biblical studies.

52 For example, William Johnsson, 'Nine Foundations for an Adventist Hermeneutic' , *Ministry*, March 1999, 14; Willmore Eva, 'Interpreting the Bible: A Commonsense Approach' , *Ministry*, March 1996, 5; or Richard M. Davidson, 'Biblical Interpretation' , in *Handbook of Seventh-day Adventist Theology*, 60. While Davidson describes the aim of hermeneutics as threefold, the two-part approach is nonetheless clearly discernable: 1. To understand what the human writers intended to convey to their readers; 2. To grasp what the divine author intended to communicate; and 3. To learn how to communicate and apply the message.

53 See, for example, Raymond C. Holmes, *The Tip of an Iceberg: Biblical Authority, Biblical Interpretation and the Ordination of Women in Ministry* (Wakefield, MI: POINTER Publications, 1994), 36. Opponents assume that what the text meant (the task of exegesis) and what it means (the task of application) are in agreement and hence both these methodological steps are rather conjoined into one. The literalistic reading tendencies also lead to a direct and immediate perception of the meaning.

54 See Gerhard Hasel, 'Biblical Authority, Hermeneutics, and the Role of Women' , 6.

Another example of how Adventist interpretative approaches generally overlap with traditional evangelical Protestant hermeneutics is represented by Bernard Ramm's *Protestant Biblical Interpretation*. The way the book defines hermeneutics as a two-stage science-art/rules-application project in the introduction, through to how Ramm organises and presents the material in its key chapters three to five, moving from inspiration to theological principles down to specific exegetical guidelines, provides a rather indicative parallel example of how Adventist interpreters define, organise and even present theological principles or specific exegetical guidelines.[55] There is hence at least a strong parallel in thinking that is discernible between the traditional two-stage Hirschian method as popularised by Ramm, Fee or Kaiser, and Adventist approaches.

A supplementary point that could be brought in to support similarities with evangelical methodology could be based on the usage of the same terminology each uses to define its methods. The suggested names for interpretative methods by Adventist scholars include 'historical-grammatical', 'grammatical', 'historical' , 'grammatical-historical' or 'Wesleyan quadrilateral'. All these terminologies are, as we have already argued, not alien to evangelical vocabulary and are descriptions of the traditional evangelical method.[56]

Adventist approaches also show general similarity to classical biblical interpretation in that they tend to under-discuss the problems of the reader's perspective and/or develop a hermeneutical theory considering the issues related to the reader's horizon.

Traditional evangelical as well as Adventist interpretations neglect to develop relevant concepts of language, meaning, the reader's understanding and pre-understanding or a theory of the role of the reader as such, as do modern hermeneutical developments. Additionally, Adventist interpretation tends to view questions of the reader's horizon with suspicion and with some misunderstandings and generally brushes them aside as being liberal expressions

---

55 Bernard Ramm, *Protestant Biblical Interpretation*. For the definition of hermeneutics, see page 1. For the structuring and specific theological principles and specific exegetical guidelines, see chapters 3, 4 and 5, pages 93-162. For Adventist examples, see particularly Richard M. Davidson, 'Biblical Interpretation' , in Handbook of Seventh-day Adventist Theology, 58-104.
56 Bernard Ramm, *Protestant Biblical Interpretation*, 114 and William W. Klein, Craig L. Blomberg and Robert L. Hubbard, Jr., *Introduction to Biblical Interpretation*, 13.

of historical-critical theories.⁵⁷ Hence there has not been a limited theoretical attempt within Adventism to engage with deeper meta questions relevant to considering the reader's contribution to meaning, understanding and generally 'hermeneutics'.

In the first section I have highlighted how leading evangelical thinkers have observed the lack of theoretical considerations themselves. Walter Kaiser has in this regard said that 'much of the current debate over the Scriptures ... is, at its core, a result of failure on the part of evangelicals to come to terms with the issue of hermeneutics'.⁵⁸ The attention of the majority of evangelical scholarship before the 1970s was on inspiration, inerrancy and generally authority of Scripture debates battling the influence of historical-criticism which meant that before the 1980s hermeneutics generally was treated rather unsympathetically.⁵⁹

At the end of this analysis, it has to be pointed out, however, that the situation in the contemporary field of evangelical hermeneutics is now changing towards a more developed and rounded exposition of hermeneutical theory which is considered to be operative behind specific applied methodological approaches. Not only the contributions of Anthony Thiselton,⁶⁰ but also particularly of Craig

---

57 Davidson, for example, treats such theoretical questions as all being part of 'The Enlightenment Hermeneutics and the Historical Critical-Method'. See Richard M. Davidson, 'Biblical Interpretation', in *Handbook of Seventh-day Adventist Theology*, 90-94. Equally, Hasel placed the questions of the reader's horizon under the historical-critical school of thought. See Gerhard Hasel, 'Biblical Authority, Hermeneutics, and the Role of Women', 6.
58 Walter C. Kaiser, Jr., 'Legitimate Hermeneutics', in *Inerrancy*, 117. Julius Scott similarly observes that 'for many evangelical Christians, hermeneutics is an area whose importance is granted but whose nature and content is little understood'. See Julius J. Scott, Jr., 'Some Problems in Hermeneutics for Contemporary Evangelicals', 67.
59 John R. Muether, 'Evangelicals and the Bible: A Bibliographic Postscript', in *Inerrancy and Hermeneutic*, 253-64.
60 Especially influential became Thiselton's *Two Horizons* (1980) and *New Horizons* (1992), *Thiselton on Hermeneutics* (2006), *Hermeneutics of Doctrine* (2007) and *Hermeneutics: An Introduction* (2009).

Bartholomew[61] have advanced the field of biblical interpretation.[62]

The field of Adventist interpretation has also seen significant advances in recent years which demonstrate willingness to engage with issues of hermeneutics, despite the fact that the predominant feature of Adventist interpretative discussions still follows the traditional text-centred and exegetical approach, which inclines to equate hermeneutics with exegesis.[63]

---

61 For example: Craig Bartholomew: *Introducing Biblical Hermeneutics: A Comprehensive Framework for Hearing God in Scripture* (Grand Rapids, MI: Baker Academic, 2015) or his latest massive multi-volume attempt, of which volume one has been published so far, addressing issues of philosophical influences within OT biblical interpretation; *The Old Testament and God: Old Testament Origins and the Question of God*, Volume 1 (London: SPCK, 2022). Bartholomew's *The God Who Acts in History: The Significance of Sinai* (Grand Rapids, MI: Eerdmans, 2020) also marks a significant contribution to the field of OT interpretation. Furthermore, the so-called Scripture and Hermeneutics eight-volume series, where Bartholomew was one of the general editors, was also a major undertaking which considered many relevant matters arising from modern hermeneutical theories. The whole series was republished by Zondervan in 2015, with the following titles: *Renewing Biblical Interpretation; After Pentecost: Language And Biblical Interpretation; A Royal Priesthood?: The Use of the Bible Ethically And Politically; 'Behind' the Text: History and Biblical Interpretation; Out of Egypt: Biblical Theology and Biblical Interpretation; Reading Luke: Interpretation, Reflection, Formation; Canon and Biblical Interpretation; The Bible and the University*.

62 Within the field of Evangelical interpretation also becomes relevant a shorter overview volume which captures the recent advances and demonstrates how the field has advanced in recent years: Stanley E. Porter and Beth M. Stovell, eds., *Biblical Hermeneutics: Five Views* (2012).

63 A number of volumes have been published within Adventist scholarship demonstrating this trend of engaging more thoroughly with the field of interpretation and also considering elements of hermeneutical theory. The most relevant of these are: Raoul Dederen, ed., *Handbook of Seventh-Day Adventist Theology* (2000), particularly Davidson's article 'Biblical Interpretation,' 58-104; *Understanding Scripture: An Adventist Approach* (Silver Spring, MD: Biblical Research Institute and General Conference of Seventh-day Adventists, 2005), edited by George W. Reid; *Interpreting Scripture–Bible Questions and Answers*, Volume 1 (Silver Spring, MD: Biblical Research Institute, 2010) and Volume 2 (Silver Spring, MD: Biblical Research Institute 2020), edited by Gerhard Pfandl; *Biblical Hermeneutics: An Adventist Approach* (Silver Spring, MD: Biblical Research Institute, 2021), edited by Frank M. Hasel; *The Word: Searching, Living, Teaching*, Volume 1 (Silver Spring, MD: Biblical Research Institute, 2021) and Volume 2 (Silver Spring, MD: Biblical Research Institute, 2022), edited by Artur A. Stele. Also hermeneutically relevant are *Scripture and Philosophy: Essays in Honouring the Work and Vision of Fernando Luis Canale*

Issues Arising for Adventist Hermeneutics

With this analysis in mind, what are the interpretative issues arising from this discussion? First and foremost, the topic of women's ordination has become a reminder that perhaps Adventist interpretation was not very successful in addressing some metacritical questions of hermeneutics. After all, Adventist interpreters have been discussing the ordination question back and forth for over a century, and both sides use the same biblical texts, yet they interpret Scripture very differently. Still, both sides believe they are following the true biblical interpretation.

Several papers in the not-so-distant TOSC (2012-2014) meetings[64] specifically discussed the question of interpretation. But a more engaging explanation as to why a specific exegetical model was proposed was lacking.

There are at least two major issues arising from the ordination debate that have direct relevance to the Adventist hermeneutical debate:

(1) Reduction of the problem of hermeneutics to exegesis (the textual problem). Most of Adventist interpretation assumes that discovering what the text meant is essentially the task of interpretation. '[W]hat the biblical text meant in principle in its original setting is precisely what the text means for us today.'[65] If this is the case, as some Adventist interpreters suggest, then hermeneutics essentially becomes exegesis with a bit of additional application attached

---

(Berrien Springs, MI: Adventist Theological Society, 2016), edited by Tiago Arrais, Kenneth Bergland and Michael F. Younker; and John C. Peckham's *Canonical Theology: The Biblical Canon, Sola Scriptura, and Theological Method* (Grand Rapids: Eerdmans, 2016).

64 Theology of Ordination Study Committee (TOSC), a body made up of Adventist scholars, administrators and lay representatives, organised by the General Conference of Seventh-day Adventists. TOSC met four times during January 2012 and June 2014 to study questions relating to ordination, the ordination of women and hermeneutics. The papers presented at the committee are available on the General Conference webpage [https://www.adventistarchives.org/about-tosc].

65 Ekkehardt Müller, 'Guidelines for the Interpretation of Scripture', in *Understanding Scripture: An Adventist Approach*, 111-34 (113). The next sentence, however, is more nuanced in its suggestion: 'Any application of a text to our situation must be tied to the original meaning' (same page 113).

to it. But hermeneutics cannot be reduced to a discussion about what guidelines should be followed to interrogate the text, i.e. basically to questions of exegesis.

(2) Reduction of the problem of hermeneutics to right attitude. The second issue arising from the ordination debate is the reduction of the problem of hermeneutics to the reader's presuppositions. It is assumed (particularly in the opponents' view of interpretation) that the key to right interpretation is the right attitude of the reader. Reading Scripture itself is not complicated, it is simple: what one essentially needs is the right attitude of faith.

There are positive signs that Adventist interpreters are actually aware of the reader's problem. An example of clearly spelling out the problem is found in Fernando Canale's suggestion that 'the task envisaged here must take into consideration three different levels of hermeneutics: (1) the hermeneutics of the text, (2) the hermeneutics of theological issues, and (3) the hermeneutics of philosophical principles ... presupposed by the exegete.'[66]

Canale's statement is one of the clearest admissions in the Adventist discussion on interpretation that there is indeed a philosophical problem with the exegete as this is beyond the issues relating to the text. They observe that both deserve hermeneutical attention, but importantly the perspective or the horizon of the reader needs to be part of the discussion, because readers are not neutral recipients of texts. There is a whole set of paradigm assumptions, cultural forces and language-communication pre-conditions which influence the formation of the understanding and meaning of the reader. The reader does not receive the textual meaning unmitigated and this issue cannot be relegated to the problem of assuming a right attitude.

Opponents particularly tend to explain the problem of the unacknowledged and behind-the-scenes operative pre-understandings and assumptions by appealing to the gaining of a right attitude of faith. With such a right attitude, interpretation becomes a matter of more or less plain reading.

Proponents, on the other hand, tend to explain the 'reader problem' by developing robust systems of rules of interpretation which ensure that exegesis will discover the original meaning of the text with scientific-like 'objective' precision. The better the rules, the better the chance there is to uncover the original

---

[66] Fernando Canale, 'Revelation and Inspiration', in *Understanding Scripture: An Adventist Approach*, 47-74 (51).

historical meaning, and that meaning is in effect assumed to control the attitude of the interpreter.

Mark Noll, however, warns evangelical scholarship that the models of their thinking about Scripture and interpretation were formed in the 19th-century milieu of the American Didactic Enlightenment.[67] The key point here is that evangelical interpretation has generalised the issue of interpretation by suggesting that the methods which current evangelical scholarship uses are essentially the methods of the Reformers.

It is true that the Protestant Reformers of the 16th century brought a paradigm shift in how Scripture is perceived and used, and evangelicalism and Adventism follow in the tradition of that paradigm shift. Yet the specific models, approaches and understanding of what exactly the Reformation's big slogans (such as *sola scriptura*) mean, what hermeneutics is theoretically and then practically, and how the reader's worldview and language function in interpretation– these were not fully explained by the Reformers in the 16th century.

In many ways Luther used the classical fourfold medieval method of interpretation, while Calvin used classical philosophers all his life to aid his interpretation. And Zwingli was heavily criticised by the Radical Reformers for not being radical enough in his sola *scriptura approach*.

We know that most of the 'exegetical' robustness of Protestant reading was based on philological models of the humanists, such as the one developed by Erasmus. Yet humanists, in many ways, held rationalistic and naturalistic assumptions. Hence, it is well recognised that Protestant hermeneutical thinking is also partly a child of humanist assumptions (as well as of Scriptural-theistic assumptions).[68]

For example, the important volume *Understanding Scripture: An Adventist Approach* (2006) only assumes, but does not explain how or why the 'historical-grammatical' method, recommended as the preferred method, is the method

---

67 Mark A. Noll, *The Scandal of the Evangelical Mind*, 83-88.
68 Stephen B. Chapman, 'Reclaiming Inspiration for the Bible' in *Canon and Biblical Interpretation* (Scripture & Hermeneutics Series, Vol. 7), 167-206 (189). Chapman writes: 'From the perspective of canonical theology, then, historical criticism and evangelicalism do not appear to be strangers to each other at all but unacknowledged bedfellows. Historical criticism is in fact exposed as a secularized version of the evangelical stance toward Scripture, with its privileging of the "original" or the "earliest" ... and its location of meaning in

that indeed arises out of Scripture. It is suggested in the volume that Seventh-day Adventism promotes 'a system of biblical interpretation derived from Scripture itself'.[69] Yet there is little explanation as to how the emergence of 'historical-grammatical' hermeneutics at the time of the Reformation is a system that has arisen from Scripture.

Now this is not a criticism against the 'historical-grammatical' method as such, but only a reflection that generally Protestant and particularly evangelical scholars tend to assume that hermeneutics has been given to them as a ready-made gift from the time of the Reformation. Yet there is very little discussion about what exactly hermeneutics was and how exactly the big Protestant slogans functioned.

Furthermore, how is *sola scriptura*, which became the main slogan of some Protestantism, related to what became known as the 'historical-grammatical method'? How do we explain that already at the time of the Reformation, Radical Reformers criticised the key mainline reformers for not following *sola scriptura*?

It has been well demonstrated that even the Lutheran programme of Reformation was not able to give the Bible to people and say to them 'read it and we will come to the same conclusions'. The 1525 Peasants' Uprising convinced Luther that people cannot just read Scripture, and that Scripture cannot interpret itself without some basic explanation about interpretation. The result was that people were given Luther's small catechism, and that provided an interpretative guide to a correct 'reader's perspective'.[70]

My research into the rationale of Adventist hermeneutics has, I hope, demonstrated sufficiently that the dynamic that operates behind Adventist interpretation is driven by fundamental assumptions about the nature of inspiration, the nature of Scripture, and consequently, the nature of interpretation as

---

the history "behind" the text. Similarly, evangelicalism reveals itself to be much more beholden to historical criticism than it realizes or is willing to concede, with its Enlightenment assumptions and empirical anxieties.'

69 Alberto R. Timm, 'Historical Background of Adventist Biblical Interpretation', in *Understanding Scripture: An Adventist Approach*, 1-14 (12, also 3-4).

70 See, for example, Alister E. McGrath, Reformation Thought, 4th ed. (Oxford: Wiley-Blackwell, 2012) and *The Intellectual Origins of the European Reformations*, 2nd ed. (Oxford: Wiley-Blackwell, 2004).

such.⁷¹ Adventist interpreters work with fundamental assumptions about these three, yet they tend not to discuss them on a theoretical level (except perhaps the nature of inspiration which has received a lot of theoretical attention in Adventism). ⁷²

If there is to be a way forward in the question of the ordination of women (and other topics), a way that is not just political or based on tolerance, but a way that is based on mutual understanding of why we have arrived at these conclusions and why others have arrived at other conclusions–a way where we move forward in biblical and hermeneutical dialogue and not toleration only– then this process should include addressing fundamental questions of biblical hermeneutics.

This leads us, then, to a very specific proposition for a way forward in Adventist hermeneutical dialogue.

The Future of Adventist Hermeneutics

Seventh-day Adventist scholarship should be alert to the fact that in recent decades there have been important changes in biblical interpretation. Specifically, the shift from questions about the original *Sitz im Leben*, which was the main concern for both historical-critical and historical-grammatical methods, to questions about the *Sitz in der Literatur*.

'Studies of intertextual relationships and those focused on the practice of "inner-biblical exegesis" have brought out stronger connections' between various genres such as wisdom, the narrative, poetic, cultic, prophetic and legal. 'What in pre-modern exegesis went under the name of the "unity of Scripture"

---

71   While I have practically demonstrated the outworking of the principle on the example of women's ordination, Fernando Canale has theoretically explained the same dynamic: 'Interpretation of biblical texts and theological issues is conditioned by the doctrine of R-I [revelation-inspiration], which in turn depends on the philosophical principles presupposed by the exegete.' Fernando Canale, 'Revelation and Inspiration,' in *Understanding Scripture: An Adventist Approach*, 47-74 (51).
72   Famously, the first edition of *Women in Ministry* does not even contain a hermeneutical chapter. However, even in volumes which do contain some sort of hermeneutical discussion, it has been mostly related to the questions of rules and models of interpretation–i.e. essentially exegesis with some theological rules, but no deeper elaboration on why exactly this approach to Scripture is taken or these rules provided.

(*unitas scripturae*) and was then largely lost during the dominance of pre-modern [Enlightenment] exegesis ... has, under changed methodological and hermeneutical presuppositions, come back into view as a space in which a polyphony of voices can be heard.'[73]

It is intriguing that even Catholic scholarship is now recognising significant shifts and developments towards a more unified hermeneutical approach to Scripture–a hermeneutics that is concerned with the concept of *unitas scripturae* as a fundamental tenet of biblical interpretation.

Frank Hasel rightly observes that '[o]nly on the basis of its unity can Scripture function as its own interpreter. Only then is it possible to come up with a harmony in doctrine and teaching.'[74] I think Hasel has put his finger on a crucial issue here. It is *unitas scripturae* that indeed is the interpretative assumption for putting *sola scriptura* into operation. This is a fundamental point concerning interpretative theory.

In other words, it is the actual interpretative utilisation of scriptural unity that establishes the principle of Scripture only. Without a hermeneutical endeavour that is capable of fleshing out the notion of scriptural unity, *sola scriptura* can be just a good-sounding slogan.

Therefore, it is my proposal that while *sola scriptura* is the hermeneutical rationale of biblical interpretation, it becomes effective only in the interpretative practice of *unitas scripturae*, i.e. made visible by an interpretative theory and model based on the unity of Scripture.

The question, then, must be asked: what interpretative model is in the best position to draw on *unitas scripturae*? Such an approach must not only attempt to harmonise scriptural passages or Bible verses in a superficial way, but it must crucially be able to compose an authentic biblical symphony out of the polyphony of voices in Scripture.

Biblical Theology as a discipline has been around for several decades, but it has only been since the 1990s that its potential to cast refreshing biblical

---

[73] Ludger Schwienhorst-Schönberger, 'Alttestamentliche Weisheit im Diskurs', *Zeitschrift für die Alttestamentliche Wissenschaft*, Volume 125, Issue 1, April 2013, 118-42. Ludger Schwienhorst-Schönberger is a professor at the Katholisch-Theologische Fakultät, University of Vienna, Austria.

[74] Frank Hasel, 'Presuppositions in the Interpretation of Scripture', in *Understanding Scripture: An Adventist Approach*, 27-46 (37).

perspectives on old debates and to move beyond disunity has been recognised. It has recently assumed the meaning of a 'discipline in the theological curriculum that views the message of the Bible holistically from the perspective of the Bible's own central theme. It is a call for the unity of the Bible.'[75]

Biblical Theology, providing a specific hermeneutical proposition, is also close to Adventist 'hermeneutical' DNA in several specific aspects: (1) In its strong focus on the unity of Scripture–*unitas scripturae*; (2) In its fundamental belief in Scripture as such–*sola scriptura*; (3) In its practical exploration of Scripture first over other sources–*prima scriptura*; (4) In its systemic use of the whole Bible–*tota scriptura*; and (5) In its belief in the possibility of understanding Scripture–*claritas scripturae*. All these are fundamental overtones of Adventist hermeneutics, but they are mostly principle statements that need practical outworking.

It is my suggestion that the traditional Protestant slogans, which are equally part of the Adventist hermeneutical DNA, namely *Unity of Scripture, Sola Scriptura, Prima Scriptura, Tota Scriptura* and *Claritas Scripturae*, are converging

---

[75] Walter C. Kaiser, Jr. and Moisés Silva, *Introduction to Biblical Hermeneutics: The Search for Meaning* (Revised and Expanded Edition), 68-69. Because the discipline of Biblical Theology has undergone massive transformation over the past sixty years, it is often mistaken for the 'Biblical Theology Movement' or more recently for 'Theological Hermeneutics/Interpretation,' or 'Canonical Theology'. While there is ongoing discussion regarding the exact nature of the methodological proposal of the discipline, in the last decade the discipline has developed much clearer contours and moved from theoretical discussion to the production of tangible results. Thus, none of the above terms describe the current state of affairs in this field. Within Adventism, apart from the involvement of Gerhard Hasel in the 1980s and 1990s, Newbold College's systematic theology pathway has been working since mid-1990s on a biblical theological proposal (for example, Jan Barna, 'The Grand Story' , *Ministry*, March 2012, 20-22, 24; and Gunnar Pedersen and Jan Barna, 'Towards a Biblical Theology Method: A 7-stage Theistic-Narrative Methodology' , unpublished paper presented at Tyndale Fellowship, Cambridge, UK, 7-9 July 2011, or Gunnar Pedersen and Jan Barna, 'A Search for the Biblical Epistemic Horizon: Towards Meta-Hermeneutics' , *Spes Christiana*, 32.2. 2021, 23-44). From within Adventist theology the contribution of John Peckham's Canonical Theology is also a relevant undertaking in this field. For a constructive discussion of and practical results in the field, see for instance the work of Desmond T. Alexander, Walter C. Kaiser Jr., Tom Holland, Christopher Wright, Graeme Goldsworthy, Craig Bartholomew, Michael Goheen, Michael D. Williams, Vaughan Roberts and Brevard S. Childs. The latest major contribution to Biblical Theology and its hermeneutical function is Craig Bartholomew's *Introducing Biblical Hermeneutics: A Comprehensive Framework for Hearing God in Scripture* (Grand Rapids: Baker Academic, 2015).

together in the discipline of Biblical Theology. In Adventism, it was Gerhard Hasel who was involved in this field. Up to this day he is still referenced in the latest books on Biblical Theology.[76] But after his untimely departure, the potentially unifying vision of Biblical Theology has almost been lost in Adventist interpretation.

It could be interesting to point out that in early Adventism Ellen White alluded to the fact that reading the Bible requires more than just 'searching out the various parts' but also 'studying their relationship'. She also implied that readers need to make 'the effort' to view individual parts 'in their relation to the grand central thought' of the Bible. Importantly, she suggested that the study of the 'great whole' of Scripture 'is the highest study in which it is possible for man to engage. As no other study can, it will quicken the mind and uplift the soul.'[77]

Intriguingly enough, White's suggestion seems to point beyond the mere compare-text-with-text methodology, as Protestantism and Adventism predominantly apply the *sola scriptura* principle. Rather, Ellen White makes a radical suggestion that readers will get the most value out of their interpretative efforts when reading the Bible as a coherent 'great whole' with a 'grand central thought'. Such an approach, as she implies, will shape the minds of readers as nothing else and it is 'the highest study' in which a reader can engage. This proposition moves far beyond what even William Miller envisioned for biblical interpretation. Yet this proposition has not yet been fully realised and integrated into the Adventist hermeneutical discussion with all its potential.[78]

---

76 Graeme Goldsworthy, *Christ-Centered Biblical Theology: Hermeneutical Foundations and Principles* (Downers Grove, IL: InterVarsity Press, 2012), see especially pages 101-104, where the whole section is devoted to Gerhard Hasel's approach to the discipline of Biblical Theology.

77 Ellen G. White, *Education*, (Mountain View, CA: Pacific Press Publishing Association, 1903), 123-26.

78 What Ellen White essentially proposed sounds very much like the most contemporary definitions of Biblical Theology as a 'discipline in the theological curriculum that views the message of the Bible holistically from the perspective of Bible's own central theme'. Walter C. Kaiser, Jr. and Moisés Silva, *Introduction to Biblical Hermeneutics: The Search for Meaning* (Revised and Expanded Edition), 68. Adventist voices raising the necessity of biblical theology include the contributions of Peckham, Pedersen and Barna or the unpublished

Conclusion

In conclusion, only a heightened awareness about the nature of interpretation and what it involves is a constructive approach for dealing with present and future Adventist controversies.[79] It is a daring road, because it will bring with it very sensitive and core issues. It is a road, however, which Adventist scholarship needs to travel.

Biblical Theology, as a middle discipline between Exegesis and Systematic Theology (and Practical Theology),[80] has potential that as yet has not been fully explored in Adventist interpretation.[81] Exploring this potential should be a natural step for Adventist interpreters, because Adventist theological and hermeneutical vision has always aspired to develop a unified biblical-theological paradigm. It would be the right step to a long-forgotten suggestion of Ellen White as well.

In conclusion, I am pleased to point out the important contribution of Gunnar Pedersen to Adventist interpretation by developing and including Biblical Theology into Adventist studies and making it an essential element of Adventist interpretation. To this end, his latest significant contribution to Adventist interpretation, 'A Search for the Biblical Epistemic Horizon: Towards Meta-Hermeneutics', is included in this volume as a follow-up chapter and as a

---

contribution of Daniel Duda, 'The Development of a Course in Biblical Theology Based on a Book-by-Book Approach to the Bible', DMin dissertation, Andrews University, 1992 (available through Digital Commons @ Andrews University: <https://digitalcommons.andrews.edu/cgi/viewcontent.cgi?article=1161&context=dmin>).

79 Jan Barna, *Ordination of Women in Seventh-day Adventist Theology: A Study in Biblical Interpretations*, 318, see also pages 308-311.
80 See the discussion, for example, in T. D. Alexander and Brian S. Rosner, eds., *New Dictionary of Biblical Theology* (Downers Grove, IL: InterVarsity, 2000); especially 'Exegesis and Hermeneutics', 52-72 and 'Systematic Theology and Biblical Theology', 89-104.
81 Anthony C. Thiselton has very favorably commented on the work of Tom Holland who is one of the leading exponents of the biblical theological approach to interpretation. See Thiselton's comments on the back of Holland's latest book: *Romans: The Divine Marriage: A Biblical Theological Commentary* (Wipf & Stock, UK, 2011). See also Tom Holland, *Contours of Pauline Theology: A Radical New Survey of the Influences on Paul's Biblical Writings* (Fearn, Tain, UK: Christian Focus Publications, 2009).

specific example of Adventist scholarship making significant inroads into clarifying and making biblical interpretation the best it can be.[82]

---

[82] Originally published in *Spes Christiana*, 32.2, 2021, 23-44.

A Search for the Biblical Epistemic Horizon:
Towards Meta-Hermeneutics

Gunnar Pedersen and Jan Barna[1]

It is generally recognised that the biblical Canon is composed of micro and macro stories but not agreed that such stories form a coherent theological narrative. While there was, in the mid-twentieth century, a renewed interest in searching for the levels of unity in the Canon, the dominant trend in biblical scholarship was the search for diversity; a search that has largely been driven by the modernist deistic and naturalistic assumptions of source, form and historical literary criticism (Kaiser Jr. 2009, 11-24).[2]

N. T. Wright argues that when it comes to recovering the meaning of the biblical texts, the 'pre-critical and modern ways of articulating this have not met with success' (Wright 1992, 122). The apparent weakness of both the historical-critical and historical-grammatical methods of biblical studies is that they both fall short of detecting the interpretative significance of the meta-narrative perspective in the biblical texts.[3] Thus the idea of a metanarrative level of unity in the Scriptural stories has generally been challenged or abandoned by the majority of scholars within the discipline of Biblical Studies.

However, more recently the proponents of the biblical theology movements called 'New Perspectives' have called for a reassessment of the hermeneutical

---
1 This chapter is republished here with the permission of *Spes Christiana*. The text of the chapter has been slightly edited mainly to reflect British spelling. The referencing style has been maintained. Originally published in *Spes Christiana*, 32.2, 2021, 23-44.
2 For an overview of the issues and challenges implied in the contemporary hermeneutical debates see: Thiselton 2009; Thiselton 2006; Thiselton 2007. See also Silva 1996.
3 For a more comprehensive discussion, see Pedersen 2016.

impasse by advocating a more narrative approach. More recently N. T. Wright, Craig Bartholomew, Michael Goheen and others have insisted that the biblical texts actually form a coherent metanarrative by insisting that the biblical stories must be understood from within their own worldview logic for their meaning to be unlocked. They insist that although the biblical Canon is the product of a long, complicated process, 'the end product needs to be examined in its own right' (Bartholomew et al. 2004, 146-47).[4]

What is gradually dawning on the postmodern contemporary consciousness is that all humans inhabit a certain worldview perspective whether they recognise it or not, a worldview that ideologically controls their interpretation of observed and experienced reality.[5] Craig Bartholomew and Michael Goheen actually state that worldviews 'offer a lens through which to view everything else'. However, such a concern for reading the Bible as a grand unified narrative mostly comes from the disciplines such as 'systematic, practical, ethics and missiology–but sadly not from within biblical studies' , except for N. T. Wright–a 'rare example of a major biblical scholar in whose work, story, in the grand sense, is central' (Bartholomew et al. 2004, 146-47).

Their thesis is that all humans inhabit a worldview paradigm that serves as the mental lens through which they observe and interpret the experienced empirical world and which informs their values and actions. Thus unless the biblical world of thought is an exception to this general cultural phenomenon, the biblical authors likewise inhabit an epistemic worldview horizon informing the meaning of their theology. In a recent series of articles the Adventist theologian Fernando Canale has called attention to the importance of the biblical metanarrative as the epistemological key to understanding how the Scriptures can yield a unified belief system. He argues that textual exegesis[6] as currently practised

---

4   The issue is that they fall short of detecting the interpretative significance of the epistemic world horizon in the biblical texts. For a more comprehensive discussion of this problem, see Pedersen 2016.

5   For a more comprehensive discussion of the role of worldviews and their importance for retrieving the meaning of the biblical story/stories, see Pedersen 2009.

6   Fernando Canale, "From Vision to System: Finishing the Task of Adventist Biblical and Systematic Theologies–Part I," *Journal of the Adventist Theological Society*, 15/2 (Autumn 2004), pp. 5-39. Fernando Canale, "From Vision to System: Finishing the Task of Adventist Biblical and Systematic Theologies–Part II," *Journal of the Adventist Theological Society*, 16/1-2 (Autumn 2005), pp.

does not uncover the biblical worldview perspective; it is uncovered through the discipline of systematics (Canale 2006, 126-38).

Canale refers to the Adventist systematic theologian Norman Gulley who insists that a canonically based systematic theology needs the 'hermeneutical guide of the biblical metanarrative' and 'worldview' for constructing a coherent belief system. Gulley thus argues that 'the biblical metanarrative operates as a guiding light orienting our interpretation of Scripture and biblical doctrine. Furthermore, it also identifies and 'corrects any interpretation that does not fit in with the biblical worldview.' Finally, 'it guides us in understanding the inner logic of biblical thinking' (Canale 2006, 135-36). Whether one agrees with Canale or not, concerning the discipline by which to retrieve the biblical epistemic worldview horizon, his core observation resonates with the emerging awareness that without discovering the biblical worldview paradigm the text will be taken captive to the worldview of the interpreter.

So, for theology to be biblical it must reflect the realities of the biblical texts including their inherent worldview. If the dominant feature of the biblical Canon is diversity and discontinuity representing multiple theologies and worldviews, any attempt at detecting a unified theology is pointless. If, on the other hand, there is an ideological and thematic level of unity in the biblical material, then a unified biblical theology appears to be possible.[7] Accordingly, the methodological challenge is to formulate a search that would allow the biblical authors to tell their own story/stories on their own terms; a method that is not controlled by the worldview lenses of the interpreter.

Biblical theology could thus be defined as a search for the epistemic horizon or worldview paradigms of the biblical authors and thus to discover what kind of 'meta-story' they inhabit and which governs their thinking, logic and interpretation of cosmos. If their worldview story is ultimately theistic, then the lens through which they see everything will be theological. Thus, to discover the 'epistemic

---

114-142. Fernando Canale, "From Vision to System: Finishing the Task of Adventist Biblical and Systematic Theologies–Part III," *Journal of the Adventist Theological Society*, 17/12 (Autumn 2006), pp. 114-142.

7   The last several decades have seen the emergence of a meta-narrative approach to biblical theology pioneered by scholars like Walter C. Kaiser Jr., N. T. Wright and others. Cf. Kaiser Jr. 2009 and 2008; Bartholomew and Goheen 2006, ix-xii; Wright 2005, 89-94; Wright 1992, 121-44; Alexander 2002 and 2008; Scobie 2003; Roberts 2002 and Goldsworthy 2012.

horizon' in which the biblical authors think, live, move and have their being is to discover their theology. Biblical theology is thus concerned with thematic analysis of the Scriptural stories as it attempts to identify the epistemic horizon of the biblical authors, to explore their logic, and to assess their narrative implications. Such a methodology could accordingly be entitled: *A Theistic Narrative Method of Biblical Theology*.

Methodological Steps

While there clearly is a growing awareness among some scholars regarding the need to recover the worldview horizon of the biblical authors and thus an increasing attention to its meta-hermeneutical significance, there is nevertheless a limited scholarly attention to the methodological process by which the epistemic worldview horizon of the various biblical authors might be retrieved, identified and assessed without imposing an alien perspective on the biblical texts. The aim of this study is thus tentatively to suggest some basic methodological steps by which to retrieve the epistemic horizon of the biblical authors and to outline its structural meta-historical implications and briefly to sketch some of its potential hermeneutical implications. We propose that the first step in the search for a unifying common epistemic horizon in the scriptural material could start with the Genesis literature by mapping out its major and minor themes.

A Threefold Foundational Perspective

In reading the first eleven chapters of Genesis it strikes the reader that it contains a unique story concerning the world and its origin. Canonical criticism does not change the fact that over time the Genesis literature became the preamble to the Hebrew Canon. Our working hypothesis is that the canonical authors could generally be thinking in terms of the triple thematic worldview perspective introduced in the Genesis literature, a worldview paradigm constituted by the following major themes, that is, a theistic creation-theme, a theistic crisis-theme and a divine remedial-promise-theme. If such a triple perspective is traceable in the plotline from Genesis to the Apocalypse, then the biblical authors share a triple epistemic horizon and thus inhabit a common unifying world-view paradigm despite any diversity.

Creation-Perspective

The *Creation-Perspective* is foundational in the Genesis story and is located as the preamble to the entire biblical Canon and apparently introduces a foundational worldview horizon within which the author understands all of divine and physical time-space reality. Thus, the most general, comprehensive, all-embracing, all-inclusive statement about everything encountered in the biblical preamble is: 'In the beginning God created the heavens and the earth' (Gen. 1:1). So if a worldview paradigm is defined as the most general and most inclusive assertion about everything, then Genesis 1:1 states its worldview paradigm up front.

The first part of the sentence thus constitutes the radical first-principle in a unique theistic worldview, providing an all-embracing view about everything. The logic of this statement is that before everything else God is. God is seen prior to everything as God is presented as the cause and originator of everything else. So the logic is that God is the uncreated ultimate dimension as everything else is seen as derived from and contingent on him. Furthermore, the next most important principle about everything is stated in the next sentence, namely that 'the heavens and the earth' are created and thus depend on the creator for their origin, order, form and structure. Thus the first statement in the Genesis account defines a unique two-dimensional universe in which there is God and creation and beyond this dual horizon there is nothing. Accordingly, the Genesis preamble defines all of reality in a single sentence.

Furthermore, this creator/creation logic implies God can be without creation as he exists prior to created reality and constitutes its pre-condition as creation itself is seen as contingent on him for its very being. The principle accordingly implies that there is an ontological and dimensional difference between God and creation. The logic of the creation statement clearly implies that nature is not self-originating or self-generating nor eternal but contingent on a theistic dimension for its origin, form, structure, function and being. Accordingly, there is an all-inclusive dependency principle implied in the Genesis formula with regard to created reality, including humans (Gen 2). The tree of life (Gen 2-3) logic implies that such a dependency is a continual existential condition.

Accordingly, the most general, comprehensive, all-embracing and all-inclusive theory about everything is stated up front in the opening sentence of the Genesis account (Gen 1:1). This theistic creator/creation formula thus provides the first principle or ultimate epistemic horizon or worldview paradigm encountered in the Canon. However, the Genesis account immediately modifies this horizon by introducing a disruptive crisis principle.

Crisis-Perspective

A second general comprehensive thematic principle embracing all of human existence is likewise stated up front in the Genesis preamble (Gen 3:8-24). A *Crisis-Perspective* appears that concerns the intrusion of a mysterious evil that radically disrupts the divinely intended Paradise order and thus God's plan for the world. While the creation story did warn against evil as a potential option, it did not present it as an inherent necessity. God is seen as giving humans a radical choice between the established Paradise order and a potential evil alternative, a choice that he upholds at all costs. The tree of knowledge motif regarding good and evil had a divine health warning attached (Gen 2:16-17). Accordingly, the crisis story concerns the fatal choice of the acclaimed progenitors of humanity.

The serpent power is depicted as a mysterious antagonistic force challenging the ontological first principles regarding God's character; a challenge that when accepted by humans will lead to fatal existential consequences. According to the Genesis account, the serpent power plants an evil idea in the minds of the human progenitors, subverting their worldview, their response to God and thus their actions (Gen. 3:1-7). The subsequent Genesis story describes how the human consciousness is altered from being in a state of mental orbit around God to an orbit around the human 'self' , leading to an accelerating state of selfishness and violence (Gen. 4-11). Human evil will thus appear as the functional result of a disrupted interactive relationship with God.

Thus, the social and physical suffering, cruelty, violence, decay and death are seen as originating in the 'fall' event and not in the created order itself. The resultant struggle between the values of good and evil is not seen as the result of an ontological but an ideological dualism in God's universe. Although physical and social evil now appear natural and normal to any human empirical observer, it is not presented in the Genesis account as something inherent to God's original Paradise order. The natural world in its current state is thus no longer depicted as only life-supporting but also as life-disruptive and even life-destructive. The state of Shalom in Paradise is replaced by deception, war, struggle, violence, suffering and death. The Genesis crisis-principle thus signals that things are no longer as God intended them to be from the beginning.

Furthermore, while the Genesis account does not explicitly explain why the deceptive event, leading to an act of defiance against God, causes physical death, later biblical authors will apparently ground this fatal effect in the human separation and exclusion from God's life-supportive presence. The Genesis account itself only depicts the radical development of human depravity through the seed-line of Cain, a story that accelerates to the point where God is seen as taking further action in terms of the challenge of evil (Gen. 6-9). So while the theistic creator/creation formula constitutes the first principle of a foundational epistemic worldview horizon, the crisis formula constitutes the central theme around which the continuing story revolves, traceable through the accelerating violence of Cain's descendants corrupting the Genesis antediluvian world. The crisis theme thus sets the stage for the third Genesis principle, namely God's dual remedial response to the crisis of evil and death.

Remedial Perspective

The third general thematic principle embedded in the Genesis worldview horizon concerns the dual *Remedial Perspective* embodied in the divine promise that God will exercise damage control by taking actions to restrain, contain and undo the evil force that now disrupts the Paradise order and thus take redemptive actions to restore humans to the Paradise life now seen as lost. The key word is 'curses' , in contrast to the preceding Paradise Blessings (Gen 3:14-19).

Curses

Thus the Genesis account indicates that God immediately takes action in response to human defection by subjecting the world to a string of natural, social, spiritual and cosmic 'curses'. Firstly, the Serpent power as the agent of human evil is unconditionally condemned to eternal destruction (Gen 3:14); secondly, as a result of the evil disruption, the male-female social relationship is radically altered (Gen 3:16); thirdly, the 'curse' is seen as resulting in radically changed environmental conditions, as humans are seen as losing their divinely given supremacy over the natural order which now turns hostile (Gen 3:17-19), leaving the created order in a state of self-regulating struggle, decay, suffering, distress and death, and finally the human interactive relationship with God is disrupted, resulting in exclusion and death (Gen 3:22-24). The Genesis story depicts God as twice taking further action, extending the physical and social curses in response to a continued growth in human violence (Gen 3:5-21; 11:1-9) and the rise of systemic organised evil. Thus, the curses appear as God's temporary damage control actions by which he seeks to restrain the human empire of evil.

Blessings

However, this is not God's only response to the rise of evil. Actually, he is seen as taking positive action, aiming at restoring the lost blessings. Thus, God is seen as simultaneously issuing a string of redemptive promises in response to the human predicament, promised divine actions that would ultimately undo the effects of evil and terminate its instigator and noting that this will happen through a human agency, that is, the 'seed of the woman' (Gen 3:15). God is thus seen as issuing a double promise to humanity to undo the serpent and all he brought to the human experience—his lies and death; a promise to empower humanity to resist the serpent power and ensure that through the 'seed' or descendants the serpent power would be destroyed. The genealogies in Genesis chapters 5, 10 and 11 are thus parading descendants who are all seen as being part of the same family line, a family story that will eventually narrow down into further subsections with Noah and Abraham. The first twelve chapters of Genesis thus logically set the stage for the Israel-centred story that follows, which in turn sets the stage for the Christ story, which in turn sets the stage for the apostolic story, which in turn sets the stage for the future restoration of all things.

Now while the overarching promise theme in the Genesis account is a victory motif, this cryptic promise does not specify how, when and by whom this will happen; it only provides a general promise that it will happen. Thus are introduced a general direction and goal towards which God will lead the human story. However, the logic of this promise is that all the evil that has been caused by the serpent-power will eventually be undone and the curses removed and the Paradise life-form restored. While the latter implications are not stated directly, the victory motif makes no logical sense if this is not the anticipated outcome.

Thus, the Genesis promise regarding God's double response logically implies that one could anticipate a God-directed story; a plot-line advancing to a divinely set goal of termination and restoration. The narrative nature of the emerging covenant story thus appears to be anticipated in the Genesis epistemic horizon itself. The subsequent plotline of the entire book of Genesis clearly follows this kind of rationale, advancing the story in stages through divine actions.

So while the theistic creator/creation formula provides the first principle or foundational epistemic worldview horizon, the crisis formula immediately modifies this horizon by adding a second principle of human evil as a disrupting and distorting force in the world, while the remedial formula provides the third principle, promising the subsequent divine resolution to the problem of evil. Accordingly, the interaction between the central crisis theme and the divine redemption theme forms the grand narrative plot-line around which the subsequent story could be expected to revolve, a plot-line advancing the drama to a divinely promised goal of the termination of evil and thus the restoration of God's intended goodness for creation embodied in the Paradise order. The Genesis triple thematic perspective has all the hallmarks of a unique theistic worldview paradigm, or epistemic horizon, and as such it would appear to provide the controlling worldview boundary within which the subsequent narratives are logically to be understood.

Tentative Methodological Considerations

The critical question concerns whether this triple Genesis perspective constitutes the worldview horizon inhabited by the subsequent Canonical authors. If this worldview perspective can be traced in the plotline from the Genesis account to the Apocalypse, then it would mean that not only do the Canonical authors inhabit a common unifying worldview paradigm despite any diversity, but they also inhabit the particular worldview of the Genesis account. In particular the dual theme of human evil and God's remedial response would serve as the centre around which the subsequent divine-human drama might be understood. Actually, the Genesis account itself introduces the reader to the first three successive historical stages in the human drama: the creation-stage, the crisis-stage, the promise-stage, a promise stage that logically anticipates an ultimate fulfilment-stage. So the story would include at least four major stages, stages that would be crucial for meta-hermeneutics.

As the first methodological step we propose the following questions as helpful in searching for the epistemic horizon within which the various Canonical authors are thinking. Firstly, there is the need to trace to what degree and in what manner the triple thematic principle is assumed, maintained, deepened, applied and expanded by the various authors of the Bible. If we find that the biblical authors think in terms of the triple Genesis first principles then we have discovered what N. T. Wright, Craig Bartholomew, Norman Gulley and others call the biblical 'metanarrative' or 'worldview' and thus their epistemic horizon. Secondly, there is a need to explore and identify the redemptive covenant promise introduced in the Genesis account, and to trace to what degree and in what manner this redemptive covenant promise is assumed, maintained, deepened, applied and expanded by the various authors of the Bible, and thirdly there is a need to evaluate the manner in which this redemptive covenant promise directs the advancing redemptive plotline through the various stages in the projected Israelite covenant history. Those critical analytical questions might help to establish not only the stages and sub-stages in the advancing story but also its worldview horizon and thus guard against imposing alien dogmatic or naturalistic assumptions on the Canonical literature. Thus the narrative Genesis logic will progressively be revealed in the advancing stages in the emerging story. Given that the Genesis account itself provides the first three successive historical stages in the divine/human drama in anticipation of an ultimate fulfilment stage, we may have a major hermeneutical key to the meaning and theology of the various authors of Scripture.

An Emerging Staged Story

The critical issue concerns the method by which this story is detected in the subsequent Canonical literature. The texts of the Pentateuch, Joshua, Judges, Psalms, Prophets, Ezra, Nehemiah, Matthew, Luke, Acts and Romans all seem to reflect a Genesis covenant interpretation of the Israelite story and even the usage of genealogies is an ingenious shorthand for linking the past and present into a coherent covenant history. Comparing the covenant interpretations of the Israelite history by the various biblical authors appears to yield a rather consistent picture.[8] Tom Wright expressed the Israelite consciousness as it matured in the hopes and expectations of Second Temple Judaism by saying that 'many first-century Jews thought of the period they were living in as the continuation of a great scriptural narrative, and of the moment they themselves were in as late on within the "continuing exile" of Daniel 9' (Tom Wright 2009, 42). In other words, they saw their covenant history as a God-directed journey extending from its perceived biblical past to its future consummation according to the biblical promise. The issue in biblical theology is not to prove that the recorded biblical history is true, but that there is a detectable unanimity in its perception and interpretation of that history and thus a common theological horizon.

Era of Promise

The genealogies in Genesis chapters 5, 10 and 11 parade a whole line of recipients of the initial redemptive promise, a promise that is seen as passing on through the descendants of Noah and which finds its constituent form in a covenant with Abraham (Gen 12; 15 and 17). The first twelve chapters of the Genesis story thus logically set the stage for the specific promise era expected to follow, which in turn sets the stage for the anticipated fulfilment era.

With the covenant charter with Abraham, God is seen as advancing the redemptive promise story through the family of Abraham as the historical human agent of bringing the promised divine blessings to the world. The covenant blessing pronounced to Abraham appears to be an echo of the primordial blessing from Paradise where it embodied the essence of God's abundant purpose for the world (Gen. 12:2-3). Thus, the story of Abraham's family is the story of God's redemptive agent of blessing in the world. The covenant charter is thus foundational for

---

8 The chronological covenant structure does not follow the order in which the various texts are located in the Canon. However, these texts implicitly and explicitly contain a historical chronology expressed by the thematic and historical markers in the text itself along with their covenant interpretation. For examples of how biblical authors think in terms of the covenant story, see: 1 Sam 12:6-12; Pss 78; 80; 83; 105; 106; Neh 9:6-37; Dan 9; Matt 7:1-17; Luke 3:2333; 24:1-50; Acts 7:1-60; Rom 11; 12; 13.

subsequent history, as God here is seen as taking action to advance his specific plan to restore the lost Paradise blessing for the world through the family of Abraham.

Thus, the Abraham story initiates a divine covenant commitment that guides subsequent patriarchal history and moves it towards the promised Exodus and beyond. The descendants of Abraham are seen as the collective seed of Abraham (Ex. 1 and 19), delivered according to the covenant promise recorded in Genesis by the specific actions of God. The Exodus event thus marks the historic action of God in directing the redemptive plotline and it was understood as such by the narrators of the alleged event. Faithful to the covenant, God is seen as hearing their cry and he brings rescue and redemption from slavery and oppression (Ex. 3; 20). The covenant consciousness about Israel's role and mission appears to be foundational for the Pentateuch projection of the future story of Israel. Accordingly, the Israelite covenant story is seen as progressing within the boundaries of God's dual remedial response to evil in terms of blessing and curses (Deut. 27-30).

The Exodus event is thus seen as God taking specific action to further advance his plan for the world by constituting the nation of Israel. Even the amendment to the Abraham covenant (Ex. 19-25)[9] with its institutions, places, objects and offices within the community of Israel is seen as an additional divinely instituted means of ensuring the mission of Israel as projected in the Covenant with Abraham (Ex. 25:8). From this juncture the divine plan for the world is seen as advancing through the turbulent history of Israel, from the time of Moses through the Judges to the rise of the monarchy, guided by the provisions of the covenant.

The appointment of David and the constitution of his dynasty as a permanent institution in Israel through a divine oath of covenant, represent a further sub-stage in the promise story. This appears as a further amendment to the constitution of Israel which fits thematically into all the previous promises, as it provides a more explicit agenda for God's plans for the world (2 Sam. 7; Gen. 17:6, 16) than do those given to Abraham and Moses. This amendment to the covenant promise will definitively shape and determine Israelite anticipations concerning God's plan for

---

9   In the comment of the Apostle Paul, the Sinai event is best understood as an amendment as he insists that whatever the Sinai covenant adds, it must be understood within the premises of the Abraham agreement. See Gal 3:15-29.

the world. From now on the idea of the kingdom, and the king as God's servant within the servant Israel, will take centre-stage in Israelite theological consciousness (Pss 2; 22; 72; 89; 110; 132).

However, the story of the kingdom after David will reveal that the kingship institution is not a cure for the problem of evil and that Israel, despite the dynasty, will continue to gravitate towards apostasy and disaster. Their history reveals that the remedial actions taken by God are apparently only provisional in nature as they are followed by a deepening crisis followed by further remedial actions. A repetitive negative drama thus unfolds through the biblical stories, reaching a catastrophic low point during the demise of the Israelite kingdom, ending in destruction and exile (2 Chr 36:11-21).

This is precisely the context in which prophets will begin to introduce a string of significant messianic-kingdom promises pointing to a 'day' when God will take decisive remedial action and thus liberate the world from the disruptive force of evil destroying Israel and the world. The prophet Isaiah in particular provides a grand vision of the future beyond the exile, a vision that will be echoed in other exilic and post-exilic prophetic writings. They will cast a grand vision of a glorious blessed future day when God will enter upon his world-wide rule through the anticipated kingship of a future son of David, who will terminate the reign of evil, restore the divine/human communion with God, spiritually renew human hearts as the precondition for a renewed creation (Isa 9; 11; 35; 42; 49; 53; 59; 65). The prophetic vision leaves the inheritors of the covenant with a massive expectation regarding a future transitional intervention in which God will eventually deliver on the promises.

God's remedial actions and prophetic promises, in response to the deepening crisis of evil in the late Israelite kingdom era, will thus generate a growing anticipation of a coming major transitional event where everything will be transformed and renewed. Thus the whole Israelite journey reveals that the Israel provisions were only temporary provisions and not the real solutions to the problem of evil. The prophetic vision of the future messianic final solution to the human predicament thus points to a coming transition point in the Israelite narrative, conceptually dividing the covenant story into two major parts, broadly defined as eras of *promise* and *fulfilment*. This, however, does not indicate that no covenant promises have been fulfilled in the past, but only that there is a significant build-up to an anticipated future transitional grand messianic event, when the problem of evil causing continued disaster will eventually be resolved, and the eternal rule of the lost Paradise blessing will finally be restored. Thus, it is the Hebrew Scriptures themselves that anticipate the coming of a future decisive transitional stage in the human story, an anticipation that was already inherent in the logic of the Genesis worldview paradigm.

Era of Fulfilment

Given that it is the Hebrew Scriptures themselves that anticipate the coming of a future decisive transitional stage in the advancing Israelite drama, the real force of the apostolic proclamation is that with Jesus the decisive transition in God's mission to the world through Israel has arrived. The Apostles thus introduced Jesus as the fulfiller of all that was promised, predicted and intended in the antecedent covenant charter and accordingly they proclaim him to be the provider of the ultimate remedy to the problem of demonic/human evil.

Jesus is presented as the promised descendant of Abraham and David (Matt. 1:1) in line with the prophetic promises. His life, ministry, death, resurrection and ascension are part of the final exodus from the continuing exile from Paradise into which humanity was plunged in the fall (Luke 9:31; John 8:33-36). Thus, Jesus is depicted as dealing not only with the temporal predicament of the Israelite nation but also with the primordial human problem of exclusion from God through the evil arising according to the Genesis event (Luke 24:47; John 8:34-36). The Apostles will argue that with Jesus the great reversal in the cosmic drama of good and evil has occurred, thus initiating the anticipated grand era of the fulfilment of God's plan for the world through the house of David. Jesus is thus proclaimed from day one on the Day of Pentecost as being seated at the right hand of God as the rightful Lord and saviour, advancing the story to its ultimate goal (Acts 1-5).

However, the Apostles not only connect Jesus with the past kingship promise package, but also present him as the one who deals with the central theme of evil as he is the one who crushes the head of the serpent (Heb 2:14-15; John 12:31). Furthermore, they explicitly claim that through his death he has resolved the exclusion from God problem, opening the way for humans to return to God (John 14:6; Acts 4:12). Christ is thus seen as the one who graciously reconnects humans to God and renews their spiritual life before restoring all things (Acts 3:21) as promised by the prophets. Given that it is the Hebrew Scriptures themselves that anticipate the coming of a future decisive transitional stage in the advancing Israelite drama, the real force of the apostolic proclamation is that with Jesus the decisive transition in God's mission to the world through Israel has arrived; the Apostles thus proclaim Jesus as the fulfiller of all that was promised, predicted and intended in the antecedent covenant history.

However, the apostolic understanding from God is that this fulfilment will not be realised as a single event (Luke 19:11) but rather in major successive stages broadly seen as an apostolic already and not yet. Thus, in the apostolic proclamation, the past and present work of the Messiah is embodied in the 'already' in anticipation of the 'not yet'. Actually, it is Jesus himself who draws this line, highlighting that the fulfilment will come in stages. More specifically, the fulfilment scheme divides the redemptive work of Christ into past, present and future stages.[10] So while the Hebrew prophetic promise story leaves the impression that when the Messiah comes everything will be restored as a single cluster of events, it is Jesus himself who claims that he as the Messiah will orchestrate this fulfilment in a series of temporal stages. In other words, the fulfilment era will also be subdivided into further stages that will be crucial for the meta-hermeneutical reading of the biblical narrative.

Thus, the drama of Jesus does not end with his death, resurrection or even his ascension. Thus synchronised with his ascension, a new stage in the fulfilment story opens. In this new apostolic 'already' phase of fulfilment, Israel is seen as being restored as a community of faith centred in Jesus Christ without the support of an earthly temple and civil state (Acts 2-4; 10; Rom 3:28-29; 9-11). The mission story now widens to include all the nations promised participation in the blessing given to Abraham. With his heavenly priestly-kingly work, Christ is thus depicted as constituting the ultimate divine antidote to the problem of human depravity as introduced in Genesis and portrayed in the biblical storyline (Gal. 3:13-14; Rom. 3:24). In this stage of the fulfilment, the newly constituted community of believers now tells the story of God's redemptive provisions for

---

10   The Apostles from the Day of Pentecost clearly distinguish between the past, present and future restorative work of Christ, thus further clarifying that the kingdom will not be restored as a single event: Luke 19:11. Acts 2:30-36; 3:19-21; 5:30-32; 17:30-31; Rom 2:16; 1 Cor 15:20-28; 2 Tim 4:1.

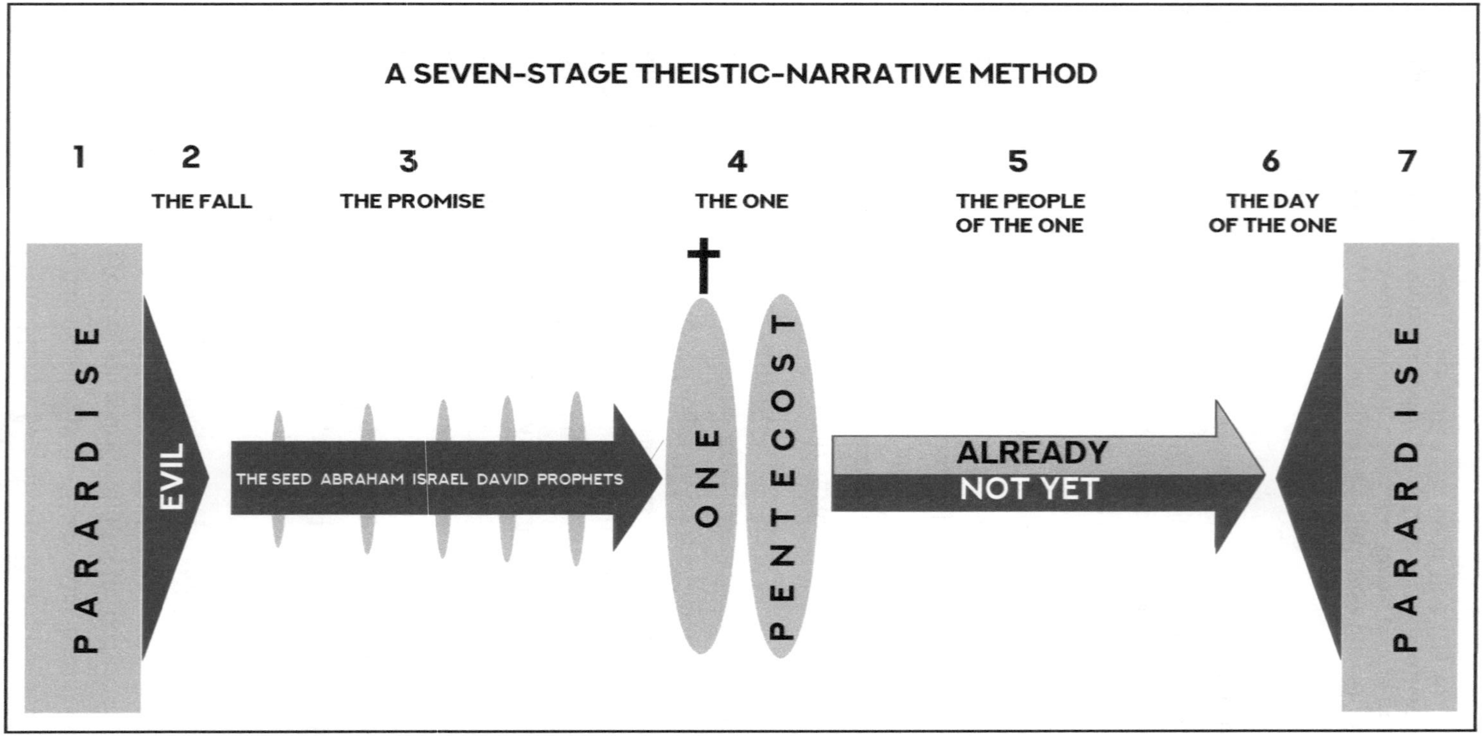

Fig. 1: A Seven-Stage Theistic-narrative Method illustration.

a fallen world and presents Jesus as the one who will be the ultimate fulfiller of God's plan (John 15:26; Acts 1:8; Rom 1:1-6).

So, while Jesus is seen leading humans into a permanent relationship with God through his priestly ministry in the apostolic 'already' of fulfilment, he is also presented as the one who in the 'not yet' of the fulfilment will lead humans into a restored new creation through his kingly ministry–that is, the shalom of Paradise (Matt 25:31-34). The Day of the Lord stage is in apostolic thinking a future 'not yet' activity of Christ in which he will fully execute his kingship as the judge of all the earth (Acts 10:42; 17:30-31; Rom 2:16). Only after the termination of evil and death does the narrative finally arrive at the stage of God 'being all' in all and thus a renewed Creation (1 Cor. 15; Rev 21-22). This is where the curses will end and sin, death and all evil will be no more, and all will be restored to the shalom of Paradise. Heaven itself is depicted as coming down on earth as God will dwell with humanity in a renewed Paradise named the Holy City (Rev 21:1-10). The exclusion from God's Paradise presence is now past and humanity will embark on its eternal journey with God, participating in his immortality (Rev 21:4; 22:1-5).

Thus, this climactic activity of Christ is depicted as the final great transitional event in the human drama, effecting the final great exodus of all humanity from the present post-Paradise state of existence. This is depicted by the Apostles, especially Paul, as the great transitional event and includes a whole cluster of divine actions such as the judgement, Christ's advent, the resurrection, the termination of the rule of evil and thus the final destruction of death, preparatory to the restoration of God's rule in all creation (1 Cor 15). While the Day of the Lord is seen as having the Parousia as its great central transitional divine act, it appears to embrace a series of pre-advent, advent and post-advent judicial activities of Christ (Dan 7-9; Rev 16-20).

Several scholars argue that the biblical covenant narrative divides into five or six major stages.[11] On the basis of the apostolic evidence we suggest instead that the covenant story may best be divided into seven major stages and that such a division will be more in line with the inner meta-narrative logic of the

---

11 N. T. Wright argues for a five-stage narrative structure, while Craig Bartholomew and Michael Goheen argue for a six-stage narrative structure of the Canonical master-narrative (Wright 2005, 89-94; Wright 1992, 121-44; Bartholomew and Goheen 2006, ix-xii).

biblical Canon seen as a whole, especially in the light of the apostolic 'already' and 'not yet' principle regarding the staged messianic fulfilment of the restorative promise. These seven major stages could be defined as follows: the creation event, the crisis event, the promise era, Jesus and the fulfilment, the gospel and fulfilment, the judgement and fulfilment, and the restoration and fulfilment.

Concluding Hermeneutical Reflections

The general pattern of promise and fulfilment and the specific subdivisions of the fulfilment principle into the 'already' and 'not yet' thus provide the reader with a major key to understanding the staged structure of the biblical covenant story, a structure that has formative implications for the exegetical reading and doctrinal application of the Hebrew and Apostolic Scriptures. So when the apostolic fulfilment story is seen as proceeding through a temporal 'already' and 'not yet' sequence, the critical hermeneutical reading issue then relates to *which aspects of the promise, purpose and predictions have already been fulfilled; which aspects are in the process of being fulfilled; and which aspects are still to be fulfilled as seen from an apostolic perspective.*

We propose that the biblical epistemic worldview horizon with its seven-staged covenant-history thus provides the necessary meta-hermeneutical controlling framework by which the Scriptures are allowed to tell their own story on their own premises. Actually, the biblical epistemic worldview horizon with its seven-staged covenant-history could be compared to a giant telescope with three sets of lenses, that is, the lenses of beginnings, the lenses of promises and the lenses of fulfilment. Thus this worldview perspective provides the mental lenses through which to interpret experienced and observed reality as it brings to view the promised divine hope for the future, a view that hermeneutically depends on the right setting of the lenses.

Accordingly, when it is textually and thematically established that a given Canonical author/text thinks in terms of the Genesis worldview horizon with its emerging stage covenant-history, then the immediate meta-hermeneutical implications are that an *antecedent context principle* must apply in the reading of that Scriptural author/text. Irrespective of where that author/text sits in the Canonical literature, one would then need thematically to trace backward in order to read the theological themes of that author/text in the light of the preceding Genesis epistemic horizon and its covenant-history and thus assess how the author/text is contributing to its vision and the advance of that covenant-history.

Furthermore, the apostolic principle of the 'already' and 'not yet' of messianic fulfilment when applied respectively to the goal of restoration and the means of restoration, will determine which elements in the Hebrew remedial institutions, practices and values have continuous validity despite temporary accommodations, and which elements will progressively discontinue and be redundant in the apostolic era of fulfilment.[12] Accordingly, then, this meta-hermeneutical principle has crucial implications not only for comprehending the continuities and discontinuities in the advancing covenant history, but also for its doctrinal implications in the advancing stages of the covenant history.

Finally, the proposed biblical epistemic worldview horizon with its seven-staged covenant-history seems to provide the opportunity for a re-mapping of the methodological process by which the reader mentally moves from text to system. Methodologically, we suggest a triple methodical process beginning with *textual exegesis*, proceeding through *thematic analysis* and ending in *systematic application*. Unfortunately the activity of thematic analysis both in part and as a whole is frequently sidelined, or neglected, and thus appears as a missing link in the mental process of proceeding from text to system. Even when thematic analysis is recognised as a necessary methodical link in the theological process of moving from text to system, it is not always granted a critical bridging hermeneutical role as a discipline in its own right. Accordingly, we propose that it is the process of thematic analysis that is the hermeneutical hallmark of the discipline of Biblical Theology.

---

12 For a more comprehensive discussion of the interpretative implication of the apostolic 'already' and 'not yet' principle of fulfilment, see Pedersen 2016, 166-74.

Selected Bibliography

Alexander, Desmond T. *From Paradise to the Promised Land*. Grand Rapids: Baker Academic, 2002.

Alexander, Desmond T. *From Eden to the New Jerusalem*. Nottingham: Inter-Varsity Press, 2008.

Bartholomew, Craig, et al., eds. *Out of Egypt: Biblical Theology and Biblical Interpretation*. Scripture and Hermeneutics Series. 5 vols. Grand Rapids: Zondervan, 2004.

Bartholomew, Craig, and Michael Goheen. *The Drama of Scripture*. London: SPCK, 2006.

Canale, Fernando. 'From Vision to System: Finishing the Task of Adventist Biblical and Systematic Theologies–Part I'. *Journal of the Adventist Theological Society* 15.2, Autumn 2004, 5-39.

Canale, Fernando. 'From Vision to System: Finishing the Task of Adventist Biblical and Systematic Theologies–Part II'. *Journal of the Adventist Theological Society* 16.1-2, Autumn 2005, 114-42.

Canale, Fernando. 'From Vision to System: Finishing the Task of Adventist Biblical and Systematic Theologies–Part III'. *Journal of the Adventist Theological Society* 17.2, Autumn 2006, 114-42.

Goldsworthy, Graeme. *Christ-Centred Biblical Theology, Hermeneutical Foundations and Principles*. Nottingham: IVP, 2012.

Kaiser Jr., Walter C. *The Promise-Plan of God: A Biblical Theology of the Old and New Testaments*. Grand Rapids: Zondervan, 2008.

Kaiser Jr., Walter C. *Recovering the Unity of the Bible: One Continuous Story, Plan and Purpose*. Grand Rapids: Zondervan, 2009.

Pedersen, Gunnar. 'The Bible as Story.' Borge Schantz and Reinder Bruinsma, eds. *Festschrift in Honour of Dr Jan Paulsen*. Lüneburg: Advent-Verlag, 2009, 237-47.

Pedersen, Gunnar. 'Towards a Scripture-Based Theology.' Jean-Claude Verrecchia, ed. *Ecclesia Reformata, Semper Reformanda*. Bracknell: Newbold Academic Press, 2016, 174-176.

Pedersen, Gunnar, and Jan Barna. 'Towards a Biblical Theology Method: A 7-stage Theistic Narrative Methodology.' Paper presented at Tyndale Fellowship Annual Conference Biblical Theology Group, Cambridge, 7-9 July 2011. Online: https://www.academia.edu/11462847/Towards_a_biblical_Theology_Method_A_7_stage_Theistic_Narrative_Methodology.

Roberts, Vaughan. *God's Big Picture: Tracing the Storyline of the Bible.* Nottingham: IVP, 2002.

Scobie, Charles H. H. *The Ways of Our God.* Grand Rapids: Eerdmans, 2003.

Silva, Moises. *Foundations of Contemporary Interpretation.* Leicester: Apollos, 1996.

Thiselton, Anthony C. *Hermeneutics: An Introduction.* Grand Rapids: Eerdmans, 2009.

Thiselton, Anthony C. *Thiselton on Hermeneutics, the Collected Works and New Essays of Anthony Thiselton.* Aldershot: Ashgate, 2006.

Thiselton, Anthony C. *The Hermeneutics of Doctrine.* Grand Rapids: Eerdmans, 2007.

Wright, N. T. *The New Testament and the People of God.* London: SPCK, 1992.

Wright, N. T. *Scripture and the Authority of God.* London: SPCK, 2005.

Wright, Tom. *Justification: God's Plan and Paul's Vision.* London: SPCK, 2009.

www.ingramcontent.com/pod-product-compliance
Lightning Source LLC
Chambersburg PA
CBHW030112100526
44591CB00009B/377